YOSEMITE

WHERE MULES WEAR DIAMONDS

BY
BOB BARRETT

COPYRIGHT 1989 by Bob Barrett
All Rights Reserved

First edition published by Loose Change Publications
936 6th St. Los Banos, California 93635

Second edition published by Ponderosa Printing
40531 Highway 41, Suite B, Oakhurst, California 93644

Third edition published by Eclectic Horseman Comm., Inc.
Po Box 174, Elbert, Colorado, 80106

Library of Congress # 89-084269
ISBN # 979-8-9893547-2-6

Project Manager: Joanne Hoefer

Graphics: Alan Marciochi

Typesetting: Tommy De Moville

Without limiting the rights under copyright above, no part of this publication may be reproduced, stored in or introduced into a retrieval system or transmitted, in any form or by any means or otherwise without prior written permission of both the copyright holder and the above listed publisher of this book.

ABOUT THE COVER: The Packers faithful friend
                    Photo by Doug Barnes

Dedication

To Joyce, my wife and friend, she made it all come true.

ACKNOWLEDGMENTS

A very special thanks to Mazie Woolstenhulme and Bill Welch who took the time to share their thoughts and memories of the past. Without them this book would not be complete.

To Jim Snyder, Yosemite Park Historian, who has spent over thirty years in Yosemite's back country, twenty four as an NPS trail worker and foreman. Jim spent countless hours reading and correcting the manuscript. He probably knows more about Yosemite history than anyone.

Jim Murphy (Cook Be Jeasus) for the oral hstory he shared that contributed so much towards the book.

Linda Eade, Yosemite NPS Research Librarian and Mary Vocelka, former librarian, who were very helpful and courteous during the time I spent in the NPS library.

Karen Wallace who spent hours with the final typing of the manuscript and offered many good suggestions towards the book.

Joanne Vanderburg of Loose Change Publishing really kept the fat out of the fire in putting this book together. Without her knowledge and expertise, this book wouldn't have gone to press.

Other people who have contributed to this book are Walt Castle, Ron Mackie, Nick Brochini, Billy Foutes, Herb Ewing, Bob Boyer, Tony DeBellis, Dick Penrose, George Meyer, Harold Hogan, Ralph and Julia Parker, Della Hern, Waine Westfall, Harold (Doc) Williams, and Everett De Moss. To all of you, I am forever grateful.

Bob Barrett

LAST OF THE BEST

Now gather round my fire boys and I'll tell you what I recall,
Of the packers in the past I knew 'em one and all.
For they could pack them terrible loads and never turn a hair,
And take those ole bronc mules and always get her there.

From McGregor, Coleman, Alvis Brown just to name a few,
And with a string of mules there wasn't a thing they couldn't do.
Louie Austen, Westfall, Burdick and Walter Castle too,
Are just a start on my list of the boys we owe our due.

It was a mid-September morning on a cloudy sort of day,
Far across the frosty meadow you could hear a pack mule bray.
The old bell mare was headed for the quakin' aspen trees,
The long earred mules a following in that cool mountain breeze.

Old Tiny was cussin' cause the camp stove wouldn't light,
He had gone and left his kindlin' on the frozen ground that night.
The boys was busy making up their loads in that early morning light,
And when the stock was gathered they would pull 'em all down tight.

I can see that picture in my mind like it was yesterday,
Of all them ole boys packing on that cold September day.
So you see my young compadres, as I tell of days gone by,
And I start to tell these stories I get a tear in my eye.

Johnny Jones, Rube, and Gilmore, Joe Barnes could stand the test,
For when it came to packing, they were part of the best.
From Reno, Allie Robinson, Woolstenhulmne and all the rest,
You boys made tracks to follow for them that live out west.

This list could go forever if I got 'em all wrote down,
And in my book they could hold their own on any kind of ground.
They're not all here with us, some have crossed that great divide,
But I thank the Lord that I knew 'em when they saddled up to ride.

                                                  Bob Barrett

Bob Mc Gregor headed for Red Peak Pass - 1939

PHOTO CREDITS

A picture is worth a 1000 words. Pictures used in this book come from several sources. Some from my own collection and others have been lent to this project by the Park Service, individuals and their families.

Maize Woolstenhulme	Meyer Family Collection
Roy Sneed	Jim Snyder
Dwight Barnes	Spud Bill
Dave Fagulia	Debbie Dalee
Bill Welch	Johanna Gehres
Tony DeBellis	Glen Fredy
Maynard Medefind	Walt Castle
McGregor Family Collection	Harvy Arancibia
Billy Fouts	Bob Barrett Collection

Yosemite Research Library

Tomoka - Bell Mule

TABLE OF CONTENTS

    Forward 8

    Introduction 11

1. Stock and Transportation 13
2. Packer Foremen 19
3. Barns 23
4. Trail Crews 27
5. Log Runs 35
6. Horse and Mule Shoeing 39
7. Forestry 43
8. Teams in the Back Country 47
9. Bridges 51
10. Packers, Mules and Hitches 57
11. Trail Signs 69
12. Women Packers 71
13. High Sierra Camps 73
14. Mounted Horse Patrol and
    Back Country Rangers 77
15. Titles and Pay 83
16. Employees and Titles 85

FORWARD

Author & String Smokey Jack - 1989

"I probably should have done things different when I was younger, but all I could see was those mules," Barrett once noted around the campfire. I doubt he would do anything different if he had it to do over. His is a life-long love affair with horses, mules and mountains, as a practiced blacksmith, horse and mule shoer, packer, and teacher, Bob is an extraordinary man of the mountains.

Bob started going to the mountains in 1948 and intends to continue packing in the Sierra at least until his 80th birthday. He learned by experience — there is very little written about packing, and that doesn't help very much when a wreck happens and you need all your wits, patience, and skill to keep the damage minimized. Bob often learned the hard way, "making do with what you got", because back in the high mountains there was little choice in the matter.

He also learned from the people around him. He enjoyed the old timers who had the skills, seeking out their friendship and experience. He has kept contact with many of them and has an uncanny ability to remember what they said and did, applying it to his own work. He is a walking encyclopedia of stories of people, the past and packing in the Yosemite region, from which he has drawn on liberally for this book. The bonds of past experience and places is a feeling for mountains and an approach to their care based on long experience of living and working in them. In large part because of his experience, Bob Barrett has become a central part of the Wilderness Historic Resources Survey conducted in Yosemite by the National Park Service with support from the Yosemite Fund.

Barrett is a modest fellow. He did not want to put too much of himself in this book, letting it honor others who had worked in Yosemite instead. "I don't want it to be a me book", he'd growl. Yet Bob has contributed to the back country lore, and some of that needs to be told. Shortly after Bob started with the Park Service, he was asked to get some grain for a mule load; he came back with a 100 lb. sack under each arm as if it was nothing. His ability to work and his integrity led him to do many things others would walk away from. There was the time a loaded mule went down in a lake while watering. Barrett jumped in to hold the mule's head to save it from drowning while another packer laughed, afraid to get his feet wet. Bob finally got the lead rope cut and the mule up. "That mule's how you make your living, McGregor told Bob; when he goes, you go." That and how you treat the land contribute to a mountain code of ethics which is close to religion for Bob.

All of this may should pretty serious, but Barrett has always spiced his experience with a sense of humor. In Jim Murphy's 1962 trail crew camp in Moraine Meadows were two young men who had gotten their summer jobs because their fathers knew the Secretary of Interior. They worked more with their mouths than with their hands. One ran track for an eastern university and had even brought his track suit. Talk around the fire generated a race when Barrett, well known locally for running as well as for letting his legs hang down, took up the challenge, winner take all. There was the college runner in uniform and track shoes down in his stance at the meadow starting line. Next to him was Barrett in Levis, a crease down each leg, no shirt, borrowed size 14 U.S. Keds, and a cowboy hat. The race was no contest, Barrett won easily. After the race, the runner's buddy a place kicker for a college football team,, suggested a kicking contest. But NPS sawyer Pete Allen squelched the contest proposing "Let's Kick a little ass instead".

The VIP's had to leave work early in the fall for school. Since the nearest road was 20 miles distant at Deer Camp, they asked Barrett if they could ride out. Bob put them on two mules in his string, padding the rough wooden pack saddles with sleeping bags. Then he took them the long way out, pretending to snooze when they complained that the forks of the saddles were beginning to settle into their rears. "The last anyone heard of them," recalls Bob, Laughing "they were walking kind of slow and standing up in the plane headed east."

Bob Barrett teaches by example, learns from those around him, practices what he preaches, and never quits doing the work himself. He believes in the lessons of the past, yet he never stops trying new things, such as trying cowboy poetry. Producing this book is one of those things. Barrett knows how fortunate he has been to have been a part of the old ways of the mountains, and he has been determined to try and put down on paper for the rest of us and for his grandchildren some of what he knows as inheritor of back country tradition about the central Sierra Nevada.

So, enjoy this book. Appreciate it as one of the very few such things that will be translated from oral history to book form. Savor the photographs of people and doings. And hope that some of what Bob has experienced will live on in the high country for the good of the mountains. Finally as Bob would say "If I don't see you in the future. I'll see you in the pasture".

Jim Snyder
Yosemite Park Historian

End of season camp move Bob Barrett, Harvey Arancibia, Frank McWhorter, and Ralph Wass

Army Packers - 1909

INTRODUCTION

From the time Indians brought them to Yosemite Valley, horses and mules have played an important part in the development of the Yosemite region.

Trade and travel occurred largely by horse and mule, in one form or another, until about the First World War. Teamsters built many of the existing roads in Yosemite. Packers supplied the maintenance and construction crews in the building of trails and bridges in the back country. Modern equipment has replaced the teamster, but men and mules continue working in Yosemite's back country today.

California's Sierra Nevada mountain range extends to the north as far as Lassen Peak and southerly to the Mojave Desert. Bordered by high desert on her east side and by rolling hills and plains on her western slope, the Sierra is a vast, rugged mountain range covered with snow for much of the year.

The Indians once used the high country as a summer home, following game to the higher elevations, gathering plants, seeds, and small game for food, and trading with their neighbors to the east. Trails to the mountains were first established by deer and other game. These are the same trails the Indians followed, and their trails established routes for settlers and stockmen in later years.

In the central part of the Sierra lies Yosemite National Park. To the majority of Americans, Yosemite means Half Dome, El Capitan, Yosemite Falls, and Curry Village, but Yosemite Valley is just a small part of Yosemite's mountain region of beauty and solitude.

With the coming of white settlers to the Yosemite region, and because of their impact on its resources, a bill was introduced into Congress in March 1864 to grant to the State of California the Yosemite Valley and Mariposa Grove of Big Trees. President Lincoln signed the bill into law on June 30.

Galen Clark had homesteaded a 160-acre tract of land near the south fork of the Merced River, providing guide and primitive hotel service to travelers to Yosemite Valley and the big trees. Clark became the first Guardian of Yosemite Valley and the Mariposa Grove.

In October 1890, Congress set Yosemite aside as a national park encompassing over a million acres. Units of U.S. Cavalry were dispatched to oversee and protect Yosemite's natural resources. The park headquarters were first established in Wawona at Camp A.E. Wood, named for the park's first Acting Superintendent.

Yosemite's back country was largely unmapped at the time. Although some trails in Yosemite Valley had been privately built, the Army started the established trail system in the back country as it is known today. A large portion of the trails established by the Army followed old Indian trails and routes used by sheep and cattlemen.

The Army used civilian packers as well as enlisted men to move supplies from one place to the next. The earliest civilian packer recorded was Gabriel Sovulewski, hired as packer and guide from April to October 1899 at $60 per month. From March through November 1901, Sovulewski was employed by the Quartermaster Department at the San Francisco Presidio as a packing instructor at $50 per month. Even before the civilian administration took over from the Army in 1915, therefore, the government stables had started to play an important part in Yosemite's front and back country maintenance and patrol. That is what this book is about.

The Indians no longer roam the high country in search of food and game. Stockmen no longer graze the mountains in Yosemite, though commercial grazing is still allowed in some Forest Service areas bordering the park. The National Park Service stables provide stock and packers for trail and bridge construction and maintenance, front and back country rangers, forestry, natural resource research and management. Hundreds of people visit Yosemite's back country annually. Backpackers follow established trails and cross-country routes. Stock parties rely on trails to reach their destinations. With this comes the history of the Park Service stables in Yosemite and its packers, mule shoers, teamsters, and trail workers.

Bob Barrett

Chapter 1

Tim Carlon

STOCK AND TRANSPORTATION

Pack stock, saddle horses, and teams were very important in the building of roads and trails in the early years. Their use today is the life line among back country trail and bridge crews.

When civilian forces took over from the Army in 1915 the NPS owned a few head of stock. Some had been transferred to the NPS from the Army, others had been purchased from private sources. Because of the many uses the Park Service had for stock, a contract was also issued to rent stock and winter pasture. Cattle rancher Tim Carlon, obtained the contract for stock and pasture rental. Carlon had land holdings in the foothills around La Grange, Snelling, and Merced Falls. He also owned Ackerson Meadow adjacent to the park and McSwain Meadows inside the park near White Wolf. He summered cattle on these ranges, which covered from Ackerson Meadow between the South and Middle fork of the Tuolumne River, Ten Lake basin to Yosemite Creek and to the rim of the Yosemite canyon, Lightning Ridge to Aspen Valley.

Prior to the NPS contract Carlon supplied horses and mules for the building of the Yosemite Valley Railroad. From September 1905 until May 1907 mules and horses were used in the moving of dirt and the grading of the railroad bed. Pack stock supplied and moved the camps in the Merced River canyon. Expert horseman Charlie Baird who worked for Carlon at this time was in charge of the horse operation.

People who knew and remember Tim Carlon, tell how he would at times ride all night, leaving Ackerson Meadow in the early evening to head for the foothill ranch, stopping at the Kassabaum ranch above Groveland to change horses. From there he rode to the Haigh or Hanlon ranches near Coulterville, where he would again change horses, so he could be on his Snelling ranch by daylight to work cattle.

Carlon's daughter, Mazie Woolstenhulme, remembers as a young girl in the late 1920'S.C., early thirties, the men coming from Yosemite to the Ruddle ranch below Snelling near the present day site of Four Corners to gather and shoe the horses for the spring drive back to Yosemite. Head Teamster, Joe Gabarnio, packers Louie Austin and Joe Rube, and blacksmith D.A. Miller were the ones who generally came. Carlon would loan out horses and mules in the winter time to local Portuguese ranchers and farmers in the area, then gather them in the spring around haying time. Sometimes the ranchers would still be using them and would try to hide them out in the willows, saying, "I can't find him, Mr. Tim". Sooner or later they would all be found.

Rancher Bill Welch, stepson of Tim Carlon, tells how Carlon would ask Miller to shoe one more horse at the end of a long day. Ole Miller, with his hat cocked off to the side of his head, would say, "Hell, I already shod twenty ranch horses for you". But he would go ahead and shoe the horse anyway. After they were all shod, the drive would begin.

Leaving the Ruddle ranch at daylight, stock were drove the first day to the Hayward ranch (Tim Erickson ranch). The following day they would gather stock around Pino Blanco on their way to the Bond ranch (near Bull Creek).

The third day of the drive would take them to Big Meadows and on to Yosemite Valley. Other years after, stock had been driven to the Hayward ranch. The second day stock would be drove to the Kassabaum ranch near Groveland. The third day more stock would be gathered at the Kassabaum and drove to Ackerson Meadow. There, stock would be separated, and those being needed in Yosemite Valley driven on. On heavy snow years stock would be driven to the Bond ranch, then down the Burma Road to Briceburg. They would follow the railroad grade to El Portal and hold them below El Portal in a fenced apple orchard (Hennis Ranch). The stock was then driven the following day up through Arch Rock into the Valley. It took several men to drive stock, but Wells Woolstenhulme, a rancher who in early years worked for Carlon and later as a NPS packer, drove over sixty head of horses and mules from Ackerson Meadows to Yosemite Valley by himself. Prior to his drive, Wells had not been to Yo-

Wells Woolstenhulme

semite Valley but he had a good sense of direction and made the trip.

Wells was one hell of a cowboy.

Bill Welch recalls during the mid-1920's of helping to drive stock up Highway 140 instead of following the railroad grade. The road was under construction at that time. Bill remembers riding around the convict workers and passing guards who were sitting on wagons with their gun and dog.

In the fall of the year when most of the horses and mules were no longer needed, they were driven from the Valley back to Ackerson, then down to the winter home range.

Some stock was kept in Yosemite Valley year round to help with winter jobs, such as the distribution of firewood, after the summer season, haul garbage and for road work. In January 1924, for example, the Park Service had twenty-nine head of stock in Yosemite Valley, 26 head belonging to the government and three to Carlon.

Of the 140 head in use in August 1924, 94 belonged to Carlon and 46 to the NPS. The total number of stock owned by the NPS would fluctuate up or down a few head until 1957, when the NPS purchased most of its own stock.

The NPS presently runs about 100 head of horses and mules. From 1915 until 1926 stock was used to work on roads both in the Valley and other areas of the park for sanitation, hauling manure and garbage, local transportation, mosquito control, wood cutting and hauling, for electrical and water system work, as well as for bridge and trail work.

Superintendents' records show that in July 1928, the NPS used a total of 173 head of stock, including 36 NPS horses and mules and 135 of Carlon's stock. The Superintendent's monthly report for July 1928 also states that a Carlon horse, a sway-backed white mare which had been used on mosquito control work at Tuolumne Meadows, was killed by falling off the Tenaya Creek trail, while being brought to the Valley by Park Ranger Adair.

When Carlon retired from the stock business in 1938, local rancher Horace Meyer received the contract to furnish stock and provide winter pasture for horses and mules. Meyers owned Big Meadow in the park as well as land around Merced Fall, Hornitos, and Mt. Bullion where he pastured for the winter.

Hoarce Meyer

Meyers and Carlon were out of the same mold; both were well acquainted with stock and hard work, both were tough old birds. NPS Packer Foreman Bob McGregor, said he never had a bad word with Meyers, and business could be done on a handshake even though the government required the formal paper work.

If a local rancher needed extra horses or mules to use during the winter months, Horace would lend them out. Meyers' winter pasture for the stock was located in Mt. Bullion north of Mariposa. During the early 1940's stock was gathered in the spring at Mr. Bullion, then driven the first day up Highway 140 toward Briceburg, where a small holding field was fenced under the grade at the site of present day Octagon. The next day's drive went up the highway to the fenced-in meadow and apple orchard below El Portal at the present day trailer court. The third day of travel took them behind El Portal up the old road to Big Meadow and Foresta. In 1946-1947 stock was held at Big Meadow, and Bob McGregor would haul the stock to the Valley by truck. In 1948 the NPS purchased a new stock truck, ending the annual drive to Yosemite. The new stock truck could haul about four head, maybe five depending on the size of the animals. When the packing season started McGregor would drive to Mt. Bullion, catch a few head, and haul them back to the Valley. In 1958 a larger truck was purchased, and six head could be hauled at one time.

Because of feed and water conditions in the fall of the year, stock at times would have to be pastured places other than Mt. Bullion. George Meyer, son of Horace, tells of taking the stock to the north side of the Merced River, above the Shilling ranch at Buck Horn. A winter storm set in late in December, he and Eddie Mankins unloaded their horses off the 49 Highway, above Bagby, in about two inches of snow. By the time they reached the higher range where the stock was the snow was about three feet deep and still snowing. They gathered the stock, drove them to Bagby, crossed the river, and went on to Mt. Bullion, a drive that was over thirty miles and colder than hell.

In the early 1950's the NPS still had a few horses and mules that had been mustered out of the army following World War II, but the majority of stock in use was owned by the contractor Meyers.

The winter of 1957 the NPS received thirty head of pack mules from the U.S. Army which was phasing out its mule outfits. These mules came from Fort Carson, Colorado by rail to Merced and then were hauled to Mt. Bullion by truck. At the time they were the finest, most uniform bunch of mules any of us had seen.

Meyers continued to supply a handful of stock to the NPS and pasture all the stock in the winter, but by the mid-1960's the NPS owned all its own stock. Meyers continued to pasture stock until 1970. He needed more room for his cattle operation; therefore the Park Service bid to other sources for winter pasture.

Below the old railroad grade between Chinquapin and Deer Camp is Rail Meadow, where the Park Service used to graze the stock in the fall of the year. During the summer months stock not in use were held here as well.

Depending on the weather, stock would be gathered around the end of October at Rail Meadow and driven to Wawona where they were held overnight before being driven 28 miles over Chowchilla Mountain to the fairgrounds in Mariposa. Shoes were pulled on the horses and mules the following day; then the herd was driven through Mariposa to pasture in Mt. Bullion. Stock were driven on the upper street of town by the court house, not up the main street. These fall drives were always fun times for the packers.

In 1963 I was a newly married man and my wife Joyce met us at the fairgrounds to help finish the drive. On the 49 Highway about where the State Forestry office is now, she and I were in the lead, and the horses were trying to crowd by. Joyce was riding an old, iron-jawed horse of Meyers that he used to run in local cow horse races. Joyce jumped out to head some of them and away they went. I didn't think I could catch that ole sorrel horse but I tried anyway. My horse swallowed his head and by the time I got things straightened out, she was already a quarter mile ahead and packing the mail.

I thought I'd be a grass roots widower, I just knew that sum bitch was going to slip on the pavement. Joyce finally got him shut off at Mt. Bullion at the pasture gate.

Because of primative road conditions and inadequate stock trucks, stock were not hauled to trailheads before 1958. If you were going to work out of the Hetch Hetchy area, you would just ride over the Yosemite Falls Trail to Harden Lake, stay a night, and go to Hetchy the following day. The same was true for any other area of the park. This was called "deadheading".

At the season's end in 1957 most of the stock were located at Harden Lake. Walt Castle and I drove them down the Yosemite Creek trail to the Valley. Several packers drove stock in the fall of 1960 from Tuolumne Meadows to the Valley via Sunrise and Little Yosemite. The fall of 1960 was the last time any stock were driven loose within Yosemite except for the fall gathers and drives out of the park.

The Yosemite Park and Curry Co., a park concessionaire, runs a great deal more stock than the government. In the fall of the year, the Curry Co. grazed their jackasses in the Little Yosemite area. They drove their horses and mules up the Four Mile Trail to McGurk Meadow, where they were held by a drift fence until feed got short. They were then taken over the hill to Fly Away, which is above Deer Camp and takes in the Turner Meadow country. From here they could graze to the Johnson Lake area. A herder stayed at Deer Camp, packed out salt, and kept strays located.

Traditionally, the NPS always waited until after the company started their fall drive before NPS stock were driven to pasture, because both parties used the same route. Fall of 1970 was the last horse drive because the NPS ended this type of grazing in the park and because Highway 49 at the foot of Chowchilla Mountain had become too congested with traffic making it difficult to handle loose stock. That practiced procedure of grazing late in the fall was good economics for an operation of this sort. Stock would be held in the mountains until early fall rains started the feed on winter pasture in the foothills.

George Meyer

Transportation costs were less than trucking, and less hay had to be purchased. The 1970 policy decision brought an end to a part of the cowboy culture that will never be again in this part of the country. Today, Rail Meadow, if you can find it, has become almost completely choked with willows and buck brush, because of lack of grazing and over protection.

Chapter 2

PACKER FOREMEN

Joe Gabarino

From 1915 to the present, there have been only three Packer Foremen in the history of the park.

The first was Joe Gabarino, whose title was Head Teamster. Not until Gabarino's retirement in 1938 was the title of Packer Foreman developed. The title change reflected changes in the use of stock in Yosemite during Gabarino's time. When he started, the barn was the hub of the whole park.

Teams of horses pulled equipment for road work, building excavation, and other work. Teamsters sometimes packed into the back country as well. Packers and teamsters supplied employees with firewood during the winter, distributing it with stock. But with the government purchase of motorized equipment and vehicles in the 1920's, which led to the development of machine shops and other specialized jobs, the emphasis at the barn changed from teams to pack stock. Gabarino's job began with a focus on front country and ended with a focus on back country.

The second Packer Foreman was Bob McGregor, a native of Hornitos in Mariposa County. Bob went to work in Yosemite as a packer in 1932. He was employed as Senior Packer until 1935, when this title was eliminated, and remained a packer until 1938. From 1938 until his retirement in 1969, Bob was Packer Foreman. McGregor knew stock and was an expert mule man. Men working under him had a world of respect for Bob, not only for his expertise with stock

Bob McGregor

but as a person as well. If he thought a packer was in the right, he would stick his head through a noose a mile to go to bat for them. His number one requirement of all packers was that the stock came first. He told me on my first day of work, "These mules are how you make your living; when they're gone, you're gone." He wanted to see them in good shape with no cinch sores, saddle galls, or hair rubbed off.

Mid-September one year Bob had hauled my stock to Hetch Hetchy. When we got to the corral area, we found that another packer had left his stock but had not made arrangements with the ranger in the area to feed while he was gone. The packer had not checked the water either, and the stock was out of both. Bob just cocked his one eye and said, "I ought to fire the son-of-a-bitch, but the season is about over. He will want a job next year, and there won't be one." That's the way he handled it. Walt Castle asked Bob once why a man never got any orders, and Bob replied, "If I have to tell you every move, I don't need you." Bob expected a man to see what had to be done and do it. If he didn't know what to do, he'd best learn quickly.

Prior to McGregor becoming Packer Foreman, a harness maker was employed during the winter months to build new pack saddles and repair equipment. McGregor assumed these duties and was an expert craftsman. He also repaired tents and ran equipment to plow snow during the winter months. With McGregor's retirement in 1969, Walt Castle became Packer Foreman, a position he still holds.

Walt was born and raised in Sonora, California. In his early years he had a paper route, delivering papers on horseback around the town. When Walt was fourteen years old, he went to work packing for Fred Leighton, which he did for four seasons. In 1951 he went to work packing for his uncle Johnnie Bonavia. The following season he packed for Cappie Cook, attending Cal Poly State University during the winter months. After serving in the armed forces in Korea, he packed for Reno Sardella from 1954 through 1956.

In 1957 Walt came to work for the NPS stables. McGregor needed another packer and old time packer Frank Coleman recommended Walt. I remember

Walt's first day on the job. At that time the Park Service had a mule called Joe. This mule had a reputation of not being gentle. Bob wanted to check Walt out, so he had Castle go to the barn, saddle the mule, and bring him down to the hitch rack. Everybody was peeking around the corner to see how Castle made out. He passed the test, and this started Walt's long career with the NPS stable operation.

Except for 1961 when Walt ran an outfit for himself and the years 1963-1964 when he worked for the Rudnick Cattle Co. in Elko, Nevada, Walt has been with the NPS. In 1965 he received a permanent position of Packer-Horseshoer. Walt also repairs all the harness and equipment, and builds new pack saddles on saddle trees made by expert craftsman NPS carpenter Horst Renmling. Walt too is an expert craftsman.

Walt Castle

Castle has always been a cowboy's cowboy and is an excellent hand at handling all kinds of stock. In his younger years he was a pretty fair hand at riding bucking horses at the local rodeos. During the years he worked seasonally as an NPS packer, Walt would ride colts during the winter months.

He also worked for the PG & E "mucking ditch", as Castle called it. When Walt decides to retire, the Park Service will lose the last of the old time hands.

Wes Wilson and Chris Brown
Indian Field Days
1st Prize - 1929

Goverment Tack Room - 1958
Bob Mc Gregor, Walt Castle Frank Coleman

Chapter 3

NPS Mule Barn - 1916

BARNS

When Yosemite was still a young national park, the U.S. Cavalry, who were managing the park, built the first horse and mule stables. In 1908 the cavalry constructed a barn on the south side of the Merced River in Yosemite Valley near Leidig Meadow. Because this site was so cold much of the year, a new barn was constructed in 1916 on the present site of the existing government stables.

The new barn consisted of twenty four tie stalls on one side with hay storage in the center and twelve box stalls on the opposite side. Mules were tied two to a stall with a pole down the middle to separate them. On the far side of the alley, directly behind the stalls, were hooks on the barn wall used to hang the pack saddles of each mule. Double doors on each end of the alley allowed for closure during colder weather, but the top door could be left open during the summer season. Stock were tied in at night, animals tied depended on the number of stock being used the following day. Hay was fed from the center of the barn and put into racks at the front of the stalls, grain was put in boxes in each stall. Excess stock kept at the barn were fed in the back corral.

Normally, young or bronc mules were tied on the right or "off" side of the stalls. A gentle mule was tied on the near side, this allowed a packer, when saddling his stock, to enter the stall on the gentle animal side.

During his tenure as Packer Foreman, Bob McGregor would tie two young or bronc mules in the same stall. He could enter those tie stalls without getting kicked or raising a fuss. I guess it appeared to the mules that he was never a threat to them. Bob was as good a mule man as I ever saw. This barn was in constant use until an arsonists fire destroyed it in 1972. That fire killed seventeen horses and mules and destroyed the tent storage shed, the shoeing shop, and tack room, a huge tool warehouse that at one time had been a mule barn. The NPS replaced this barn on site with a much smaller version which is in use today.

Hay for the barn was cut from Yosemite Valley meadows in the early years and during the summer months the NPS would pasture their stock at night in El Capitan Meadow.

During the 1924 hoof and mouth outbreak, special permits had to be secured from Federal officials to move any stock. Therefore, all stock needed for the season were moved to Yosemite at one time instead of bringing them in as needed. Larger numbers of stock early in the year over grazed the fenced pasture in El Capitan meadow. A herder was put with the stock during the day to graze the outer boundaries of the meadow, returning the stock to the fenced pasture at night.

The old tack room in Yosemite Valley was built at the same time as the barn. There, personal riding saddles were kept, harness was repaired, and mules were packed. Bob McGregor, raking rocks around the hitch rack, would say, "I wish you fellows would either learn to pack or pack these rocks out of here, so I wouldn't have to be moving them all the time". A packer coming into the valley would often slip a rock under the lash rope to balance a load that had started to slip. Over the years you could have built a monument at that old tack room with all the rocks brought in. Nobody claimed them; nobody would owe up to the fact that they had to use them, but they got there just the same, and McGregor would haul them off.

A small barn stands at the edge of Miguel Meadows and was originally built by Miguel Errera, early day cattleman. This barn, on the National Register of Historic Structures, is used by NPS rangers and packers for grain and tack storage. A small corral adjacent to the barn is used for wrangling stock. The NPS constructed a small barn at Tuolumne Meadows in 1924. This barn consisted of four tie stalls on each side with an alley down the center and a hay loft overhead. A small tack room was constructed in 1930. The barn and tack room have been used primarily by rangers. NPS packers working out of the area stacked their tack outside and covered it with a tarp. The Park Service moved the old Tuolumne Meadows fish house to the corral area in

1961, and now serves as a tack room for NPS packers.

A wrangle horse was kept up at night and all stock was turned loose in the meadows to graze. Because of increased auto traffic in 1956, a fenced pasture was built on the river across from the ranger station and barn. The Curry Company in early years grazed their stock at Dog Lake in a fenced pasture left over from the days of the Cavalry. In later years before the moving of their stables to its present site, they grazed the stock up the Lyle Canyon. Today all stock is kept in corrals and fed hay, transported in by truck.

NPS corrals at Hetch Hetchy are in the old rock quarry left from construction of the dam. A small shed for tack and hay storage sits on a flat rock overlooking the reservoir.

Mather ranger station, built in 1933, has a small barn and fenced pasture. A small barn and corral at Wawona, built in 1941, was used primarily for ranger stock but was removed in 1970.

Southeast of Chinquipin at the end of the old Sugar Pine logging company railroad grade, lies Deer Camp. A cabin, barn, and corral were built in 1916 as a ranger outpost. Through the years it was used extensively by trail crews, rangers, and BRC crews as an easy access to Yosemite's south end.

Packers coming in for supplies would stay overnight in the cabin, and stock would be turned out above the barn and corral in a nice meadow. It was handy and used extensively from 1916 to 1970 when the NPS removed these structures.

Property at Big Meadows acquired by the NPS from local rancher Hoarce Meyer in 1974 has two large log crib barns standing unused at the edge of the meadow. These barns were made of hand hewed logs and the structure was known as the Mormon Pole Barn. Another barn of this type stands at the site of the old McCauley ranch. It is also unused today. The barns at Big Meadows are the oldest barns standing within the park boundaries, built somewhere around 1870. The McCauley barn was built in 1883. Other barns in the park are those of the concessionaire Yosemite Park & Curry Co. Their largest barn is in the floor of Yosemite Valley near Curry village at the site of the old Lamon homestead and apple orchard. Other company barns have been built at White Wolf, Tuolumne Meadows, and Wawona.

Where the Ahwahnee Hotel now stands, the Coffman and Kenney Company barn once stood. Frank Coleman told of packing from this barn in 1915, hauling cement to Soda Springs in Tuolumne Meadows for the construction of Parsons Lodge.

Barn at
Miguel Meadows

Burro Pass - 1957
Packer Murphy

Trail Camp - Matterhorn Canyon

Chapter 4

Bee Hive Trail Camp - 1956

TRAIL CREWS

There was little difference between trail and road work in Yosemite Valley when the State managed that part of the park. Crews ditched the roads and trails spring and fall, patched walls and trail tread, brushed, and laid riprap on the roughest sections of trails. After the national park was established in 1890, the cavalry blazed and mapped trails, hiring contractors for much of the actual trail work. About the time Yosemite roads were paved, trail and road work separated into different skills. Under the cavalry administrations, most of the trail network of Yosemite as we know it today was established. The heaviest trail work continued to occur in Yosemite Valley where the Tenaya Zigzags were built in 1911. After the National Park Service was organized in 1916, rebuilding of Valley trails began with longer switchbacks and lower grades, work depending heavily on support of pack stock and teams.

In 1917 the construction of the Tuolumne Canyon Trail between Harden Lake and Glen Aulin began. Interrupted by the First World War, completion of the last stretch of this trail through Muir Gorge began in 1924 with two crews of a dozen men each. One crew worked from the Tuolumne Meadows side and the other from Pate Valley. Several seasons of hard work were necessary to complete this trail, after which work shifted to construction of new bridle paths in Yosemite Valley and reconstruction of the Four Mile Trail to Glacier Point. In 1930 construction began on the new Nevada Falls Trail from Clark's Point through Lost Valley and on to Merced Lake. Depression halted trail work except for some minor maintenance until 1938 when the Isberg Pass Trail was started, followed in 1940 by the Red Peak Pass Trail through the Clark Range. Since then the only large scale new trail construction has been the trail between the Sunrise High Sierra Camp and Echo Valley in 1960.

The building of the Red Peak Pass trail was a major trail building project with a construction crew on each side of the divide in 1939 and 1940. One crew was camped on the west side of the pass above timberline at Upper Ottoway Lake, where they remained until the trail was completed. On the east side of the pass, the first camp was at Triple Divide. As the trail was built toward the pass, the camp was moved to the trail crossing of the creek flowing out of Edna Lake. The third and final camp move was just under the pass at over 10,000 feet elevation. Louie Austin was the packer for this camp; he packed on the job site and moved the camp. Wells Woolstenhulme packed the supplies for the camp from Yosemite Valley, a long, hard ride of over 30 miles in rough country. Alvis Brown packed supplies from Yosemite Valley to the Ottoway camp.

Trail crew foremen on the Red Peak Pass construction were Art Watson and Fred Dresslern. Other workers were Harold Hogan, Bob and Vern Boyer, Paulie Westfall, Lloyd Bays, Dan Howard, Lawrence Ashworth, Dan Branson, Merrill McNally, Angle Roan, Hank Dryer, and Nick Brocchini. Nick Brocchini remembered that, when he was working in the camp on the Ottoway side, a young man he bunked with got a bad nosebleed one night. Crew members thought he might die, so they put this fellow on a horse, and Ed led the horse afoot.

When they got to lower elevations the young man began to feel better, but Nick went on to Yosemite Valley with him, walking 28 miles that night.

Back country trail crews have often been divided into two categories, maintenance crews and construction crews. Maintenance crews move more often, camping a week or two in the same place.

Louie Austin - 1931

They generally brush the trail, clean waterbreaks, and fix rough spots in the trail by laying short stretches of riprap. Construction crews remain in an area longer to do the extensive work required in the reconstruction of a trail or the complete building of a new one.

Maintenance crews were smaller in size, generally consisting of eight men: five laborers, a foreman, cook, and camp packer. These crews would generally move every two to three weeks, depending on the workload and number of trails in the area. The main considerations for the campsite were available feed for stock, water, wood, and access to work. In some places where there was little feed, along the trail up the Tuolumne Gorge for example, the packer would set up a separate camp to hold the stock, complete with anvil and crude shoeing platform. Feed was packed to the camp in such situations. In fact, the velvet grass in Pate Valley came from the packing of hay around 1920 to crews building that trail.

Construction crews were larger and sometimes spent most of the season in one camp. In the 1970's the California Conservation Corps sent trail crews to work with the NPS on several reconstruction projects. These CCC crews had between 17 and 24 men and women in each camp. It took between 32 and over 50 mule loads to move these camps. Because of their size, these camps were less mobile and moved less often, doing more reconstruction than maintenance work.

Maintenance crews most often moved with 10 mules, but the larger camps took 17 to 20 mule loads to move. The packer in camp would take five mule loads over to the next campsite the day before the initial move was to start. The following day another packer or packers would be sent out to help complete the move. These packers were known as camp movers. During Bob McGregor's tenure as Packer Foreman, it was a standard practice to hold over and rest the stock after a hard or long camp move.

The camp packer would come out once a week and bring back fresh supplies and the camp mail. When not hauling supplies or moving camp, the packer would haul rock and pack dirt on the trail, brush the trail, or cut wood for the cook.

Each camp had three 12' x 14' canvas wall tents, one for the cook and two for sleeping quarters for the crew. A canvas fly suspended on poles in front of the cook tent provided cover for the workers as they were served breakfast and supper family style on a table constructed of poles and covered with a top made of canvas and wooden slats. Lunch material was set out on one end of the table, and workers made their own lunches and packed them out on the job in cloth sacks hung on their belts. Seats around the table were cut logs, made from down timber.

Every season trail cook Tiny Taylor would construct an easy chair for himself, making it from small limbs and hand-hewn shakes. This chair was traditionally put on top of a pack and hauled from camp to camp. The cooks cooked over a woodstove. A screened meat safe was hung on a pole suspended between two trees to hold fresh meat and some perishables. A quarter of beef was received weekly for the camp, along with ham, bacon, fresh fruit, milk and eggs, fresh vegetables, and canned goods. The cook would bone that quarter of beef as soon as it got to camp because meat will start to sour around the bone first. Steaks were cut and hamburger was ground by a portable meat grinder. Toward the end of the week the rest of the meat was made into a roast to prevent spoilage. The meat was kept in the meat safe, hung from a pole to allow air to circulate around it. The screen kept the flies out. By being hung high in the air, the safe discourage the bears somewhat from an easy meal. Some of these meat safe poles can still be seen today around back country campsites, remnants of days gone by. Fresh milk and some types of vegetables were put in the creek in a metal container; the cool water flow was nature's refrigerator. Today there are only two men left with the NPS who can run and maintain a camp in the old way. Jim Murphy, a seasonal, has worked trails for thirty-one seasons since 1951, and Jim Snyder, Park Historian, has worked trails for twenty-four seasons since 1962. Propane stoves and refrigerators have replaced the woodstove and meat safe in present-day back country trail crew camps.

Tiny Taylor - 1962

The cook was generally up about 4 a.m. starting his fire and preparing breakfast, which was served at 7 a.m. The cook tent was off limits to everybody unless invited in by the cook. A jungle fire was situated not far from the cook tent. This fire heated all of the camp's hot water. Water was usually heated in two 30 gallon garbage cans, though in earlier years copper boilers were used. Early risers who wanted to warm themselves or have coffee before breakfast would build a fire and make the coffee in the camp coffee pot which was always on hand by the jungle fire. A stake driven in the ground nearby provided a rack for the crew's coffee cups. Through the 1950's each cup was handmade out of a tin can with a copper wire handle and hung on a nail driven in the stake.

A wash rack was built just behind the jungle fire, where wash pans were available for hands, face, and shaving. A dipper hung on a nail to take water out of the heating cans. I can remember as a green kid getting my ass chewed out by trail cook Tiny Taylor for not using the dipper. I had used a wash pan instead to dip water, but I never made that mistake again.

In the days before garbage was packed out, trail crews would dig a large pit about four feet deep just outside the camp, and all the garbage and trash would be dumped into this pit. Bears often fed in these pits, which kept them out of the camp kitchen. On camp moving day this pit would be burned, then filled back in. In the late 1960's trash was burned in the jungle fire before being packed out. In 1972 crews began using portable hot wires to prevent bears from entering the cook tent.

All trail crew members walked between camps, but the cook traditionally rode a horse or mule. Packers helping with the move brought a mount for the cook. The saddle the cooks had to use was an old army McClellan, worse than riding a pack saddle. The cooks as well as the cavalrymen must have been iron clad to sit in one of those all day.

Trail cooks were very important in holding a camp together because hard working men needed the best of food to do a hard day's work. The cook also set the standard for camp sanitation. The list is endless of the good cooks who came and went, and then there were others who did not stay very long.

Roy Marchbank was camped at Half Moon Meadow in the early '60's and was having a rough time getting a good cook to stay in the mountains. Trail boss Doug Thomas had just sent one in to replace the cook who had just quit, and it was during the moving of this camp to Ten Lakes that things went to hell.

The new cook, whom everybody in the crew knew only as Rose, would cook breakfast the night before so he wouldn't have to get up so early the following morning. He also washed the dishes in cold water. The morning after the camp move, Roy asked Rose, "What is your full name?" "Jessie Grant Rose," he replied. And Roy said, "Jessie Grant Rose, pack your bags. You're going down the hill."

During a camp move and after the camp was completely torn down, the trail crew members would head out for the new campsite. A couple of crew members would stay behind to rake and clean up the old camp after the packers had loaded up and left.

In camp the stock was always belled and turned loose to graze. Grain was packed in to grain the stock morning and night. This helped keep them nearby, and the stock would usually come into camp about daylight for a bait of oats.

Yosemite's north end provides a somewhat easier place to hold stock. With its steep, narrow canyons, short drift fences and trail blocks make it difficult for stock to leave. In Yosemite's south side, a less rugged terrain makes it easier for stock to work around drift fences. Because of the terrain, there are also fewer fences there.

Stock as a rule will start to drift about 30 minutes prior to daylight, so a wrangler has to be out of the blankets early. Mosquitoes will cause stock to leave if the infestation is bad enough. As a rule stock will work high to get the morning's first sun. It is not uncommon for a packer to walk a couple of miles to find his stock in big country. There are some horses that just do not like to stay in the mountains and will quit you first chance they get. On occasion a packer will lose his stock, leaving him afoot with a lot of hard walking miles ahead of him. After losing his stock one time, Waine Westfall noted, "There isn't anything more pitiful than fat horse tracks going down the trail ahead of you."

Roy Marchbank, trail crew foreman during the '50's and '60's, was camped once at Merced Lake. On completion of the trial work in that area he was waiting for a packer and orders from Trail Supervisor Doug Thomas to move camp. After a couple of days and no word, Marchbank indulged in the spirits, walked to the Merced Lake Ranger Station a couple

Roy Marchbank - 1956

hundred yards away to phone Thomas at his home at 2 a.m. in the morning. At that time of the morning, Doug wanted to know what in the hell Roy wanted and, after finding out, told him there would be a packer in the following day. "Is there any damn thing else you need?" Roy answered, "Yes, send me five gallons of table wine and a white tablecloth." Thomas and Marchbank were always bantering one another, but it was all in good fun. Marchbank would send the time slips, grocery order, and mail out weekly with the packer, addressing it all to "Dog Thomas". Doug would send all information back addressed to "Roy Mudbank". They were friends and got a kick out of harassing one another.

During Doug Thomas' tenure as Trail Supervisor, he spent a great deal of his time in the summer months in the back country. He knew the condition of the trails in all parts of the country and where the work was needed most.

He would never announce to the various crews that were out when his arrival might be. He might ride in five minutes to quitting time or at two in the afternoon. He felt this way he kept everybody honest about their work habits. One time a crew had given him notice that they were ready to move.

When Thomas came in, he was not satisfied with the completed trail work and had them start over to bring it up to standard. His main concern on trails was the High Sierra Loop and all trails in and out of the Valley as these were the ones most used by visitors and the concessionaire.

In the spring of 1956 I was cutting logs off the trail with sawyer Snuffy Butler and was working out of Bob Barr's camp in Little Yosemite. The first morning in camp about daylight I was thinking about getting up and wrangling the stock when I heard the bells coming into camp. They got louder as they got nearer. I pulled back the tent flap to see packer Murphy catching up his stock, so I just settled in the blankets for a while longer.

Pretty soon the bells sounded like they were leaving camp. I got up in a hurry. Murphy had caught his stock but didn't catch mine. This was his way of educating a young kid to help share the work load and to take care of his own stock.

Stories are still told about "Spud" or "Packer Murphy", whose real name was Forrest Murphy. He packed for the NPS for a lot of years. He was a rough talking old cuss but was good hearted to everybody, and his bark was bigger than his bite. He knew the mountains and took good care of his stock.

During the time Snuffy and I were working out of Barr's camp, we ran across a big Jeffrey pine that had fallen across the Panorama Trail the previous winter. It was on the Nevada Falls side about a half mile above Illilouette Creek. We didn't have enough saw to cut the tree, so we decided to use dynamite to blow it. Packer Murphy was the powder man, and we took two cases of powder with us. We cut a couple of notches in the log on each side of the trail and loaded 'er up. Snuffy went down the trail to Illilouette Creek to stop any hikers from coming through. Murphy rolled out about 50 feet of blasting wire and got behind a tree on the uphill side. I took the stock up the trail to get them out of the way and to stop any foot traffic. I no sooner got around the bend in the trail when Spud touched 'er off. My horse spooked and the mules tried to run off. Snuffy got showered with rocks at the creek crossing, and the windows at the Glacier Point Hotel damn near shook out. It took us the rest of the day to fill the hole in the trail and clean up the mess. The concussion was so bad the scrub oak trees around the blast for 30 yards were stripped of their leaves. The blast made a pretty good racket in the floor of the Valley, and we caught a lot of flak over it from the NPS brass. I think that was the end of Packer Murphy's career as a powderman for the NPS.

The use of dynamite in trail work is often essential. The older powdermen often learned their trade in the mines before coming to the park.

If a trail crew did not have a powderman in camp, the crew foreman did the blasting. Packers bringing explosives in put the dynamite on one mule and the blasting caps on another; you sure didn't want to mix them. After the mines shut down, trail crew people learned to handle explosives from more experienced powdermen in the field. Today, regulations require anyone handling explosives to attend a blasting school for one week and to work with a certified blaster for some time after that. Upon successful completion of the school a card is issued that has to be renewed every three years for packers and blasters as well.

Trail crews used hand steel with single- and double-jacks to drill holes for powder as late as 1958. In 1930 the National Park Service purchased a Rix Trail Compressor to run a jackhammer which was last used in 1957. Walt Castle and I packed it out of Union Point. It was a bastard to pack, weighing over 200 pounds and round shaped, making it very difficult to balance. Because of its weight, it had to be packed on top of the mule. I wanted to roll it over the cliff, cut a lash rope, and tell Thomas we lost it in order to save a mule. Walt decided it would be best to pack it out.

Difficulty in packing meant this generator was used very little for back country trail work. In 1957 the NPS purchased a new Homelite generator to run the jackhammer. It weighed about 150 pounds and was much simpler to pack.

The Park Service purchased a Cobra jackhammer in 1960. This self-contained hammer is a single piece of equipment with a starter rope like a chainsaw. The Cobra was used for drilling dynamite holes and supplanted hand drilling. Still, the Cobra was not used often and many crews got used to bulldozing with powder rather than drilling for it in the 1960's. The Cobras were difficult to keep running well. One crew in 1973 raced the Cobra with hand steel and beat it. They used hand steel with plugs and feathers to cut rock that summer.

In 1974 the Park Service purchased the first Pjonjar jackhammer. These Swedish hammers ran better and were tougher under back country conditions than the Cobras. Easy to pack, they came into frequent use on Yosemite trail crews, more to cut rock than for blasting. Wilderness Utilities supervisor Sonny Lawhon has kept them in good repair since they first arrived.

Chapter 5

LOG RUNS

Bill Sabo - 1978

Cutting logs off the back country trails is commonly known as "logging", and the trips to log the trails are "log runs". A packer and sawyer (a woods worker) with two saddle horses and a string of five mules to carry their camp and equipment go into the back country to cut and remove logs off the trails from the previous winter. When working out of the floor of the Valley or other areas close to roads, only one mule is needed for the saw, fuel, and other equipment. At times, wet winters, high winds, and avalanches can cause havoc to the trails. Being among the first out each year, logging crews often give first-hand reports of trail conditions.

Prior to 1950, when chainsaws were introduced to the park, logs were cut by hand, using an axe or crosscut saw. In some cases dynamite and black powder were used. Even after saws were introduced, explosives were sometimes used to camouflage the saw cuts.

The powderman really had to know his business and be very precise with his powder. A notch was cut in the log on each end, a few feet back from the trail. Powder was placed in the notch and covered with dirt or mud, then detonated. If too little powder was used the log would just splinter, and a time-consuming job of cutting the rest of the log out with an axe was at hand. If too much powder was used, a large hole might be blown in the trail, and that would sometimes take a day to fix. Often a packer would have to use his mules to haul rock to fill these holes. Another problem with powder was that, during dry months, the fuse detonating the cap could start a fire when concussion from the blast threw the still burning fuse into the brush or timber. Early day packer Bill Welch told of carrying blasting caps behind the cantle of his saddle, thinking that, if they were put on a pack mule, the pack might hit a rock or tree causing the caps to go off. I guess they didn't think of the saddle horse falling or some other type of jar that could set off the caps. The caps could blow one heck of a hole in the back of your saddle, among other things.

With chainsaws, trails can be opened more quickly to cut down on erosion and impact from rerouting around windfalls. Using chainsaws is a much quicker and more economical and environmental way of logging trails. In the mid-50's a young sawyer went out with packer Alvis Brown. The young fellow didn't like to stay in the mountains, so, in about two days, the chainsaw would break down and they would have to come back to civilization to fix it.

After the second breakdown, Alvis never said a word but tied a crosscut saw over the pack. That was enough to keep the chainsaw running for the rest of the log runs.

When trail crews used to work six days a week, a packer and sawyer would stay out from 12 to 14 days at a time, working Sundays as well. These crews came out only for groceries and fresh supplies when needed. The Sunday you worked, you took off later. You always worked from sun up until dark, stopping early if good horse feed was available. You didn't have to worry about violating the Fair Labor Standards Act, and for back country work it was a hell of a lot better that way.

Early in the spring at the end of March, weather permitting, a log crew would log all the trails in the floor of Yosemite Valley and work the trails leading out of the Valley until meeting deep snow. That completed, log crews would move to the Wawona area and follow the same procedure, always pushing the snowline. This time of year weather could be very adverse, and it was not uncommon for crews to work in the snow and rain. After Wawona, crews then moved to Hetch Hetchy and continued to log trails there to the snowline. Doug Thomas, Trail Supervisor during the 1950's and early 1960's, always wanted the trails around Hetch Hetchy opened as far as the snowline by the opening of trout fishing season, about mid-April. When crews got finished in the Hetch Hetchy area, the spring thaw was usually in full swing, so crews could advance farther into the back country.

It would take most of the summer season to completely remove all logs from the trails. If the winter brought deep snows, high Mono winds, and Avalanches, two logging crews might be employed, one in the north end and one in the south end of the park. Records show that the seasons after 1937, 1950, 1955, 1963, and 1965 floods were some of the worst years for log and trail damage. Ordinarily the entire network of trails in Yosemite were completely logged each season, but that practice has not been followed in recent years.

During the flood of 1955, high winds prevailed in the back country with wet conditions and heavy snows. After the flooding, the high country trail system was a mess with downed timber. During the month of June 1956, a log crew cutting out of the Deer Camp area made only about 3-1/2 miles to Turner Meadow. The log jams they cut through in the red fir forest stood well over a man's head. Trail crew foreman Jimmy Jones, working out of Deer Camp, had to use powder to blow these log jams in order to cut them safely. By July 4th, his trail crew was able to move to Crescent Lake by skirting around down timber that lay in the trail.

Working out of Jimmy's camp, the log crew then cut back towards Deer Camp to complete the job. On a section of trail in the Soda Springs area of Givens Creek, 89 logs were recorded cut on a one-mile section of trail. Fire and avalanche could also produce high numbers of logs to be cut. The 1966 Echo Valley fire left many snags which fell in 1972 so that log crews had to cut through 110 trees to the mile on the Merced Lake trail.

In the first part of August 1956, Superintendent John Preston, with his party and packer Waine Westfall, were in the Benson Lake area where the trail was completely plugged from the Piute Creek crossing to the campsite by the lake a mile away. Upon his return from the trip, Preston instructed Trail Supervisor Doug Thomas to supervise personally the trail cutting operation at Benson Lake. Thomas and packer Harvey Arancibia left Tuolumne Meadows around August 20th, headed for Benson Lake. Sawyer Snuffy Butler and I left from Harden Lake via Pate Valley about the same time to meet Thomas and Arancibia at Benson. It took one and a half days with two saws and four men to clear that mile of trail.

Upon completion of the Benson Trail, Thomas and Arancibia left for Stubblefield and the Jack Main Canyon which had not been logged yet. Thomas had a report that the Rancheria Creek Bridge was out and sent Butler and me via Seavey Pass, Bear Valley, and Rancheria Mountain to investigate, opening the trail as we went. Two days later, about 4 o'clock in the afternoon, we came to the spot where the bridge should have been; sure enough, it was out.

Not wanting to backtrack, we slid off the side of the mountain and hit the old Army trail that took us to the old crossing at City Camp. After untying the mules from one another, we took off our boots and forded the stream leading the stock one head at a time through boulder-filled Rancheria Creek.

From there it was about three miles to Tilltill Valley. We cut that trail out and arrived in Tilltill about 9 p.m. I always figured afterwards that Thomas already knew the bridge was out. By Labor Day that year all the trails in the park had been cleared of logs.

Bill Sabo was probably the best sawyer in the park. Sabo came to Yosemite from the East where he had been a tree trimmer after the war. He began working for Forestry in 1950, then switched to the Trail Office in 1959. I went on many a log run with Sabo. He was very particular about his equipment. If he hit dirt or cut a rotten log with his saw, he would stop immediately to resharpen it. He didn't invent the chainsaw, but he did refine its use. Around camp in the evenings after a day of cutting logs, he would walk up the trail two or three miles to check for logs so he could anticipate the workload for the following day and figure his cuts.

Harvey Aranciba - 1961

In 1964 Sabo logged the entire park trail system by himself. Bill also cut and replaced many of the trail bridges in the back country, priding himself on efficient use of on-site timber and the low cost of replacement.

Bill lost his life in a boating accident on Mono Lake in September 1978. After he died, Julia Parker said, "He's not dead. He's in the willows." When crews are cutting a large windfall or through avalanche areas, he is probably laughing his tail off. We try to cut it to the standards he set and hope he would be proud.

Chapter 6

HORSE & MULE SHOEING

NPS Blacksmiths
Fred Bruschi & Darl Miller

Early day horseshoeing came under the direction of the blacksmith. The blacksmith's duties in Yosemite during the era of horsedrawn equipment were the repairing and building of wagons, scrapers, and wheels. He also made and sharpened tools. If the smith needed a tool or special device, he simply made it. Along with these duties, the blacksmith was the horseshoer. Until 1926 the NPS kept around 40 head of stock on the Valley floor during the winter months. With the passing of horsedrawn equipment, the blacksmith spent the winter mainly sharpening hand tools and drill steel, shoeing horses and mules in the summer. From 1916 until 1938 the blacksmith would travel in the spring of the year with the packers to the foothill area around La Grange and Snelling to shoe the horses and mules as they were gathered off the winter range in preparation for the long drive to Yosemite. Because of the length of the drive, unshod horses would become sore-footed. By the late 1940's, when the trucking of stock had replaced the stock drives, all stock were shod on the floor of Yosemite Valley at the start of each season.

The original blacksmith shop, built about 1916, stood roughly above where the NPS wearhouse now stands. In 1936 a large building was built to house the carpenter, plumbing, electrical, sign, and other shops. The machine shop and firehouse were there as well as the new blacksmith shop.

Because this new shop was some distance from the barn and corral, stock were led across the maintenance yard to the shoeing shop, taken inside, and shod. Even the gentle stock did not like to stand inside this building.

There was too much commotion from the other shops. About the time a shoer was getting under a horse or mule, some damn fool would stick his head through the door of the shop and spook the animal, causing it to set back or jump away or on you. Not all of the stock were pets; Frank Coleman always said, "I saw one mule that wouldn't kick and he was dead.", and Walt Castle would add to that, "There are two kinds of people who shoe mules — the quick and the dead." If a person worked around the shop very long and had any religion, he would soon lose it as pleasantries more often than not filled the air.

A set of shoeing stocks used to shoe rough horses and mules remained in this shop. They were a holdover from the days of the Cavalry. These stocks are now in the Pioneer History Center at Wawona. During his tenure as Packer Foreman, Bob McGregor would not allow anyone to use them. He said, "An animal won't learn anything in them, and, when you have to shoe someplace besides the Valley, you can't take them with you anyway." So foot ropes were used in place of the shoeing stocks, and most everything had to have a leg jacked up to be shod. As a rule all young and hard to shoe mules were first worked a couple of weeks to take the edge off of them before shoeing.

Paco Harlow - 1987

While horseshoeing continues, blacksmithing is no longer needed because the park uses ready-made shoes and parts, and because the tendency is to buy a new tool rather than to fix an old one. Until 1965, everything was shod out of a fire. The heavy steel shoes were put in a forge, heated, shaped, and the heels cut off to fit. Through the late forties until 1965, a shoeing book was kept on all horses and mules. A shoe was fitted to a horse or mule and a diagram of the left front and hind shoe was drawn in the book. A horseshoer that was going to shoe ranger or packer stock at a trail head or ranger station out of Yosemite Valley would look at the diagrams of the stock he would have to shoe. He then would shape the shoe, cut the heels to fit, and backpunch the nail holes. This was all done the day before to save time, The day the shoer left the Valley he would load the forge, anvil, shoes, nails, and all of his tools in a pickup truck and drive to the place he was to shoe. When the shoeing started he lit the forge to heat the shoes as all that was needed in the final fitting of the shoes were minor alterations. Areas that stock were shod out of Yosemite Valley were Tuolumne Meadows, Wawona, Mather, Hetch Hetchy, Migel Meadow, Crane Flat, and Deer Camp. This book was destroyed in the barn fire in 1972.

In 1959 a new shoeing platform with open sides was built above the mule barn. This move came about when the Road Department's new office cut the blacksmith shop in half, which didn't leave the shoer much room to work, let alone to walk behind some of those cranky mules. Waine Westfall, shoer at the time, said, "Some of the brass making the mule orders should try and work in here." This new shop was a lot handier because it was close to the corral. Horses and mules being shod could see their partners in the corral.

It was also cooler and had less people traffic. These shops all had wooden decks to shoe on. This last shop was destroyed in the 1972 barn fire.

Shoeing in the Valley today is done alongside the existing barn rather than in a special shoeing shop.

From 1916 to 1930 Fred Bruski was head blacksmith for the NPS. He had men in the shop under him working as blacksmith's helpers. Frank Hendrick was employed as a horseshoer in 1918 under Bruski. Other men working as horseshoers under Bruski were Dan Garvie in 1925 and Joe Barnes in 1930.

Upon Bruski's retirement, Darl Miller was hired as head blacksmith. In 1931 four men were employed as horseshoers working under Miller: Joe Barnes, John Peters, Bill McDaniel, and J.H. Johnson. In 1932 Barnes and Peters were both retained as horseshoers under Miller. Miller held the position of blacksmith until his retirement in 1945, after which the permanent position of blacksmith was no longer filled. A couple of the welders in the NPS Machine Shop had extensive blacksmith and some stock experience, however, Bill Kirk and Sid Carter continued to do blacksmith work to make parts for antiquated back country equipment.

Horseshoeing was done under the title of blacksmith until 1959. Shoers working under that title were Theodore Sidor in 1947, Harry Thatcher in 1948, Bob Ryan in 1949, and long-time cattle rancher Clair Wolfsen between 1950 and May 1956. Waine Westfall, packer for the NPS since 1949, became the blacksmith in 1956. He held this job and title until 1959 when a permanent position for a horseshoer became available. Although the title for this permanent position was "packer", the job was primarily to shoe stock.

Waine Westfall - 1954

Westfall still worked as a packer on occasion, but he spent the winter months in the blacksmith shop sharpening tools and working for Roads in snow removal. Waine held this position from 1959 to June 1963. With the untimely death of Trail Supervisor Doug Thomas, killed in an auto accident, Westfall was put in charge of Trails. I received the position of permanent packer in January 1964, and resigned in March 1965. Walt Castle next held the position of permanent packer from April 1965 until November 1969, when he became Packer Foreman upon Bob McGregor's retirement. In 1972 Rick Watson was hired to fill the position of Packer-horseshoer, which he held until 1982, when he transferred to Teton National Park. Today, this position does not exist.

The horseshoeing is done by Paco Harlow on a seasonal basis. Today, as in the past, packers who are capable of shoeing help the horseshoer from time to time. Packers are required to be able to shoe in the field. Some of them carry the tools of the trade and a stalljack in the back country to keep their string shod in rough country. When a stalljack is not available, shoes are crudely shaped on a granite rock.

Blacksmith Shop - 1934

Chapter 7

Everett De Moss - 1959

FORESTRY

Park Forester Emil Ernst made a back country reconnaissance in September 1935 looking for evidence of needle miner and bark beetle infestation of forest trees in Kerrick Canyon, Bear Valley, Benson Lake, Rodgers Canyon, and Cold Canyon. He saw little infestation on the trip.

This same year the first bug control program started in Yosemite's back country. A stub crew of seventeen CCC workers were packed into Little Yosemite Valley to battle bug-infested trees. Before 1935 all bug crews had worked from roadside. Records state that after sixteen work days these seventeen men had covered 1700 acres of rough country, treating 60 Jeffery Pine, 55 Lodge Pole, and 3 Sugar Pine trees. The following year bug crews returned to Little Yosemite and by August completed their work in this region. Their camp was then moved to the Illilouette Creek basin.

The records do not mention any back country bug work during the forties, but in 1950 Ernst made another trip to Kerrick Canyon and other areas he had visited in '35 and '36. He reported no needle miner infestation in Kerrick, but in the Spiller and Conness Creek drainages infestation was raging. Some of the ghost forest present today are remnants of these infestations.

Everett DeMoss grew up on a ranch in the White Rock area of Mariposa County and came to work for the NPS as a packer in the spring of 1950. Everett is handy with stock, can operate heavy equipment, and is a top tree man, blacksmith, and carpenter. He is now stationed at Hodgdon Meadow as a foreman. His first two weeks as an NPS packer were spent packing for trails, after which he packed for the Forestry Department where he remained. In 1950 and 1951 he packed for Blister Rust Control crews on the middle fork of the Tuolumne River, packing from the Tioga road. In 1953 he packed from Baseline out of Mather to the Smith Peak area, and in 1954 he packed out of Deer Camp to a crew camped on Chilnualna Creek.

In 1954 a crew was packed into the Conness Creek basin by packer George Calkins, beginning the control of the Mountain Pine Beetle in the north end of the park. The method of control was to fall and burn the infected trees.

June 28, 1954 was the best work day that summer with 128 trees being treated, according to forestry records. This area has since grown up with reproduction, but the dead fall looks like a war zone.

In 1956 a bug crew returned to Little Yosemite. DeMoss was packer and camp foreman with Frank Coleman packing as well. In 1957 DeMoss was packing and supervising a crew in the Delaney Creek region.

In mid-May 1959, DeMoss and myself packed a camp and crew of thirteen men into Delaney Creek. This camp remained on Delaney Creek for five weeks, workers working seven days a week. The chemical "Lindane" was used for the first

NPS Bug Crew - 1959

time to replace the burning method. Trees were felled, limbed and bucked, then sprayed by hand with the chemical. This chemical was packed from Tuolumne Meadows in 5 gallon cans, four to the mule. Three packers, Bud Rickey, Steve Wight, and Spud Murphy worked out of the camp, hauling the chemical to the workers in the woods.

The following year camp was again set up on Delaney Creek. Bug work continued in that area and extended to Dingley Creek. One fellow packing out of the camp got lost all the time, he wore his spurs upside down, and the boys on the crew called him "Jingles". Expert tree men Charlie Castro and Jay Johnson were doing the tree falling on this project. Charlie came riding into camp one afternoon leading the mules, and Jingles was walking behind.

Charlie said "the son-of-a-bitch can't find his way back to camp, he needs to walk". Gib Douglas was the cook for the camp and you always had pies and cakes with your supper. Portable showers were packed in, and it was a first-rate camp. Other crew members were Paul Thompson, Benny (Chee) Begay, Leo Livingston, Howard Yanish, Tim Myer, Ron Wilson, John Leonard, Clyde Foley, Ernie Wass, Gil Hall and George (Pop) Albeck.

This was the last pack camp in the back country for the NPS Forestry Department. In 1962 the NPS supplied the stock and packer for a Forest Service bug camp on Indian Creek across from El Portal, and later that year another camp was put on Bishop Creek. This brought an end to all NPS involvement with stock in the back country bug work.

Robert L. Barrett, author's father
Moranine Meadows - 1951

Yosemite Historic Research Survey
1989
Bob Barrett - Jim Murphy - Jim Snyder

Author packing up

Russ Tanka - 1989

Chapter 8

Walt Castle with Team - 1957
Shoes & Beck

TEAMS IN THE BACK COUNTRY

With the coming of the automobile, the use of stock in the maintenance and construction of roads came to an end. Teams continued for a while to play an important part in trail and bridge work in the back country.

Mules were used in the back country for teams because they could be worked as pack stock when not in harness and because they were more versatile to the job compared to horses. In bridge or trail work, a team of two mules were used when there was room, but often only a single pulling mule was possible. Ed Bowman, Carpenter Foreman from 1933 to 1954, was an expert bridge builder and could handle a team as well. During the 1940's and early 1950's, he used a single mule named Dick to skid bridge stringers into place.

For changing the wood stringers to steel above Tuolumne Falls on the Glen Aulin Trail in October 1957, a team of mules, Shoes and Beck, were used. They were referred to as the "Mutt-and-Jeff team", one large and the other smaller. A log puller was placed under a heavy steel stringer to make skidding easier. These two mules, both broken to harness but of unequal size, made work difficult because the larger mule Beck would hit the collar and back off about the time Shoes would try it. I can still see frustrated Walt Castle throwing the lines 20 feet in the air and hollering, "Billy Jesus!" After a fashion the two mules got to working together, and the job was completed. Frank Coleman, an old time packer and teamster, was working on the job and gave lots of good advice. Before the mules started to work as a team, he would look at one of them and say, "I think I'll kill you and tell God you died natural."

From the late '50's to 1974 teams were used sparingly in the back country. As trails deteriorated, however, the use of teams was reintroduced to back country work with new methods of trail repair and reconstruction.

Packers most often served as teamsters. To leave the packer free to pack, trail crew foreman Jim Snyder started driving mules himself under the direction of Walt Butler and Walt Castle. Snyder started driving a single mule and, where room allowed, working a complete team. Jim took an interest in his work and became a top hand at driving them. His first team was a pair of mules, Katie and Belle, who had originally been broken to harness pulling logs in the swamps of Arkansas. These mules weighed around 1100 pounds each and pulled well together, winning several blue ribbons for pulling at Bishop Mules Days. When not used as a team, they often packed dirt and rock.

In summer 1975, Snyder and his crew constructed a trail causeway across an eroded meadow at Tuolumne Pass below Vogelsang, working back toward Rafferty Creek. A single mule in harness (Katie) was used by Snyder for this project.

Jim Snyder with team Tinker & Tanker

Tim Ludington and his trail crew worked in the falls of 1983-1985 to complete this project, building a total of a mile of trail causeway to eliminate meadow ruts and erosion in Rafferty Meadow. I call this section of trail the "stairway to heaven". Packers Craig Ritchie, Jamie Watts, and Billy Fouts did the teamster work for Ludington. Adverse weather conditions late in the fall made for difficult working at this high elevation; snow and wind forced closure of the camp in the fall of 1983.

In 1976 Snyder's team was Tinker and Tanker, two Belgian mules weighing about 1400 pounds each, who had spent their early years working for the Amish. These mules had some age on them, but Snyder learned how to care for them and pulled with them several seasons. These mules had not previously been broken to pack and reluctantly performed that particular job.

A stoneboat is used to skid rock to the job site on back country trails. In the 1920's a trail stoneboat was often made with wood cut on site and fitted to metal parts packed in. In 1973 Bill Sabo found a stoneboat made of x 2-1/2' x 5' piece of steel weighing 300 pounds which had been used in building the El Portal Road. In 1975 the welding shop made a lighter one weighing only around 150 pounds. These stoneboats were packed as a top load; the much heavier one was traded off between mules as it was packed in.

In 1974 packer John Moe used a rented team of horses and a Fresno scraper to dig the settling ponds for the Sunrise High Sierra Camp sewage system. When the NPS reconstructed the sewer system at the Glen Aulin High Sierra Camp in 1984, a team of mules and a Fresno scraper were used to move dirt for the sewer mound. The following year the same type of job was done at the Merced Lake High Sierra Camp. Billy Fouts, NPS packer since 1982 with team experience before working in Yosemite, han-

"Pet" carrying a 300lb stoneboat - 1974

dled the teamster chores on these two jobs.

Driving a team in the back country is unlike working one on the flat terrain in the valleys, where level and flat surfaces are normal and hazardous objects do not frequently appear. Steep hillsides laden with rocks, trees, brush, gullies, and streams make everyday teaming in the back country careful and interesting.

The Belgian team of Mark and Scott used at Merced Lake by Billy Fouts were a strong team weighing about 1400 pounds each and had been known to take a hike with teamsters like Snyder in the past. Because of the amount of gravel needed for cement work on this project and the distance from its source to the job site, the packers made a portable wheeled dump cart to pack in from Yosemite Valley and assemble on the job. The cart allowed quicker, more economical moving of gravel than by packing on mules.

Now this cart had a hydraulic brake system. Packer-teamster Fouts decided that riding the cart would do much to save his legs, since walking behind a team all day had a way of wearing one down. He employed the service of long time trailer worker Russ Tanaka to ride shotgun and be his brakeman.

Late one afternoon, while Billy and Russ were riding the cart back empty, Mark and Scott began to pick up a little speed, and soon it was an all-out runaway. Billy was laid back on the lines and screaming for Tanaka to pull the goddamn brake, but Russ, a-grinning, had already bailed off. The team went down through the trees, packing the mail, hit a waterbreak, turned the cart over, and put Billy in orbit. The team ran off to the area where they had been fed and harnessed, and stopped. Such wrecks are not common occurrences during the everyday work schedule, but Billy got plenty of teaming experience in a very short length of time.

John Moe, who had worked for the NPS in the mid-70's and again from 1986-1988, grew up working teams of horses on his father's ranch. John was an expert teamster and had the ability to break young stock to harness. Always laughing, John did a lot of the teamster work during the time he worked for the Park Service.

Because of economics and less impact to the environment, and as long as there are back country trails, teams will still have a job to do. Their continued use, however, is dependent on keeping the old equipment and handing down the skills of driving teams from one generation to the next.

Before

eroded meadow

After

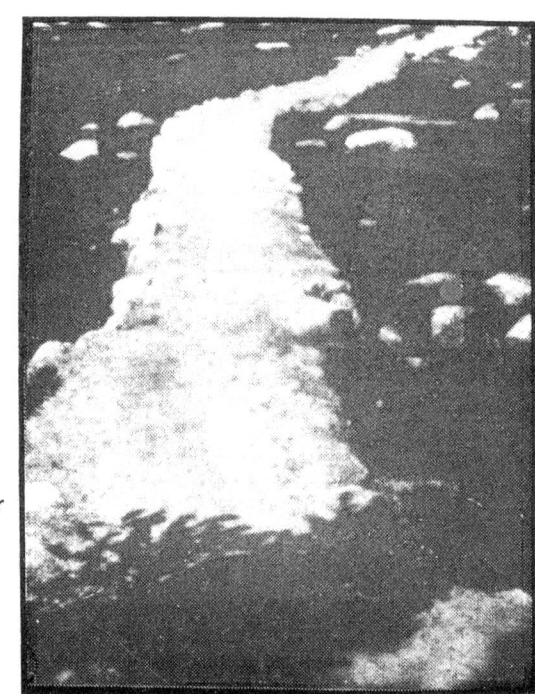

Stairway to Heaven

Chapter 9

Prefab Wood Bridge - Rancheria Creek - 1988

BRIDGES

With the building of trails came the building of bridges. In the early years of the National Park Service, bridge maintenance and construction came under the carpenter shop and was supervised by the Trail Department. For a short time in the early '30's, bridges and trails were supervised by district rangers. Carpenter Foreman Ed Bowman was an expert bridge builder in charge of these bridge crews. Bridges were built from raw material obtained on the bridge sites. The crew, camps, and equipment would be packed to the site, camp set up, and construction would begin.

Until chainsaws were introduced into the park, all trees were fallen with crosscut saws, often called "misery whips" by the workers. The logs were bucked to their proper lengths, and axemen would hand hew the logs into stringers with broad axes and adzes. These stringers were usually cut a year in advance to allow them to season because green logs would sag and sometimes twist. A team of mules or a single mule in harness would skid the stringers into place with the aid of snatch blocks. A highline of cable was put into place to lift the stringers across the stream to abutments made of rock or rock and cement.

Sometimes in falling, a tree would take an unexpected twist and break shorter than the length needed. Sometimes part of it could be salvaged for decking. An expert with trees and saws, Bill Sabo cut a complete bridge for the long span in

Pate Valley from a single large yellow pine in 1965.

In heavy snow years high water during spring runoff would sometimes take bridges out, and others, in time, would have to be replaced because of dry rot. When crews were not replacing bridges or putting on new decking, they were checking bridges for damage and dry rot, fixing bridges as needed. This practice of bridge maintenance ceased in the early 1950's, bridges being replaced only as they went out from high water or as dry rot got them.

Mule packing 14 ft. section bridge steel

In 1937, the Vernal Falls bridge stringers were replaced by steel, and in 1940 steel was added to the Nevada Falls bridge. Fourteen inch I-beams 35 feet long were taken to these bridge sites with a small tractor. The steel beams were then camouflaged with half logs cut on site, bolted to the outer side.

As timber because scarce on some bridge sites and Ed Bowman's skills were lost, prefab steel bridges were introduced in 1961 to the park bridge system. The first prefab steel bridges were made by the Bailey Bridge Co. of San Luis Obispo. Three of these bridges were made to go to Echo Creek on the newly constructed trail between Sunrise High Sierra Camp and Merced Lake, Tiltill Creek in Hetch Hetchy, and Illilouette Creek.

The steel stringers for these bridges were 14 feet long and two of them made a load of 300 pounds per mule. Because of their length, the gentlest of mules had to be used to pack these stringers. A packer could only handle two mules safely at one time, leading one mule and turning the other mule loose to follow. These mules got pretty good at handling this steel. If they hit a rock or tree, they would stop, back up a step, then go on. These bridges were not really made to pack on mules, but they were packed anyway.

The first bridges to be packed were headed for Echo Creek from Yosemite Valley. Because of the long distance, the bridges had to be packed in relays. The stringers were taken to Vernal Falls Bridge by a small tractor, then packed from there to Little Yosemite. Bill Sabo helped me pack these bridges to Little Yosemite. When all the steel had been hauled to Little Yosemite, a camp was set up for the packer and the second part of packing began to Echo Valley. A trail crew was camped in Echo Valley, and packers stayed in the trail camp to pack the bridges on the last leg to the bridge sites on Echo Creek. Waine Westfall, Steve Wight, Harvey Arancibia were other packers who helped pack these first bridges.

Walt Castle rolled a string of mules loaded with camp supplies. The trail was then changed to a more practical grade, a big help during the packing of the bridge steel.

Jim Murphy was bridge crew foreman on the upper Echo Creek bridge. A highline was put in. A section of bridge was built, shoved out on the highline, then

Nevada Falls Bridge - 1941

Abutments for the bridges on Echo Creek had been put in the previous year when the trail had been constructed. Instead of engineering and surveying the trail out, Trail Supervisor Doug Thomas and Park Engineer Bob Fleming just went through the country tying ribbons on the brush to mark the trail route. The trail as marked was so steep that packer another section added, and then the bridge would be ready to drop in place on the abutments. But as the bridge was being shoved out over the stream, one of the shallow-rooted red fir in the rocky terrain started to pull out. Murphy ordered another 100 feet of cable so he could tie that tree back to another one. I was packing for the camp at the time, and when I returned to Yosemite Valley, I asked Doug Thomas for another 100 feet of cable. He informed me, "They don't need any goddamn cable." So when I arrived in camp the next day Murph asked me where the cable was, and I said, "You don't need any goddamn cable." Murphy and his crew added another section to the bridge and started to shove it out on the highline. Louie Coleman said, "It ain't going to hold, Murph", and into the drink she went.

Doug Thomas rode up about that time madder than hell but didn't say too much. He sent me back to the Valley to get some big jacks and more cable for a new highline. The bridge was jacked up on cribbing cut from small logs placed underneath. Despite some lost time the bridge was eventually put into place. The trials and tribulations of this bridge construction led to quite a party there; for years afterwards the place was fondly remembered as Whiskey Flat.

At Tiltill Creek in the Hetch Hetchy area, a steel bridge of the same size was ferried across the reservoir on the City of San Francisco's boat to Omaha Beach, a level place near Rancheria Creek appearing when the reservoir is low. From the beach it was a short pack of about 1-1/2 miles to the bridge site.

Omaha Beach is just a rock pile, without any trees to tie the stock to while packing. A lash rope tied around the middle of a large boulder served as the hitch rack. It was early April when the packing of this bridge started and it took one week to pack the stringers. Barnium Bennett and I were camped on the bank of Rancheria Creek at City Camp, about two miles above the beach. It rained about every day and it must have been raining in the high country as the lake was rising between two and three feet a day. We didn't have a tent in camp and to keep our bed rolls and camp gear dry, we covered everything with tarps. We would to go bed in the evening with the chickens just to get warm. The crew that were hauling the steel across the reservoir would just dump the steel stringers at the edge of the water. In the morning when we rode down to the lake to start packing, all you could see of the steel was the orange shining under the water. One of us would pull off our boots and wade out waist deep, bend over and tie a rope onto the stringers and then snake them out with a saddle horse. Rain gear didn't help much, we were wet assed all day. The last bridge of this type was packed from Glacier Point 2-1/2 miles to Illilouette Creek.

In 1962 these steel bridges were modified and Western Consolidated Steel Co. of Fresno was awarded the contract. The new stringers were eight feet in length and were therefore much lighter and easier to pack. You could get over rougher trails with the shorter stringers, and they did not have to be relayed. A packer could handle a full string of mules instead of just two as with the longer steel.

The first bridge of this style was built at the Silver Apron on the Merced River above Emerald Pool and Vernal Falls. Bill Sabo, Louie Coleman, and my father were on that bridge crew. They tore the decking off the existing wooden bridge and built the new steel bridge on the old wood stringers. When the bridge was complete, Sabo cut the stringers out from underneath the new bridge with a chainsaw, dropping the new steel bridge in place on the abutments. This set a precedent for future steel bridge installations.

Western Consolidated bridges were also packed to Twin Bridges, Echo Valley, Alkali Creek at Glen Aulin, and Falls Creek at Hetch Hetchy. Ralph and Kenny Wass, Max Cheshier, Waine Westfall, Harvey Arancibia, and Walt Castle all packed these bridges.

Ralph Wass and I were camped at Hetch Hetchy in the fall of 1963 and packed the five steel bridges that went in on Falls Creek. Bill Sabo, Louie Coleman, and Eugene Sneed were the crew that installed the bridges. It was late in the fall when the bridges and decking were completed and in place.

The heads of state decided to put Premix on the bridge decking to help preserve it. The Premix was dumped beside the Lake Eleanor Road where the Falls Creek trail leaves the road. It was snowing a little each day and because of the cold weather the Premix was like concrete. Ralph and I would pick a hole in the Premix, pour diesel fuel in the hole and light it afire to try and warm it up and make the shoveling easier. After loading it on the mules and packing it to the

Author crossing Pate Valley Bridge - 1989

bridge, it came out of the dirt boxes like a brick. The bridge crew somehow got the asphalt spread over the decking. The covering of the wooden decking with asphalt may have made the deck last longer but it sure was rough on chainsaws when the deck had to be replaced.

The advantage of a steel bridge is relatively little maintenance. Once in place, unless high water takes them out or heavy snow loads bend them, they virtually last forever. Decking has to be changed periodically because it has a tendency to rot or wear in time even though the wood is treated.

When a steel bridge is washed out or becomes badly twisted, it is difficult to remove. A cutting torch has to be packed in to cut the bridge up into small lengths so it can be packed out.

In 1986 the first prefabricated wood bridge was packed and put in place on Rancheria Creek above City Camp in the Hetch Hetchy area. This was the first bridge of this type to be introduced into Yosemite's bridge program, and it may well become the bridge of the future for Yosemite's back country.

Maynard Medefind - 1973

Chapter 10

PACKERS, MULES, AND HITCHES

Loading the camp stove

Old time packers Frank Coleman and Reno Sardella both said, "If you can pack for the National Park Service in Yosemite, you can pack anywhere." They said this because the heavy construction material and equipment that had to be packed for crews in the back country and the ruggedness of the country meant that a packer had to learn quickly and well to last.

In the early years equipment used for packing was limited mostly to pack bags (kayaks), slings, and pads made from bunk mattresses. Boxes made of plywood fitted into the pack bags. The mattress pads could be rolled and put on top of the pack boxes to allow the stove load to clear the saddle forks. Powder boxes were sometimes used to build a platform for top loads such as the stove.

Two holes were cut in the center of the mattress so that the cut-outs fitted over the forks of the saddle with the sides hanging down to protect the mule's ribs and hips from long side loads. Pipe steel or lumber sometimes was packed with ends down in the pack bags and crossed over the back of the mule, secured to the forks of the saddle. A box hitch was then tied over the load. This load had to be tied extra tight because this top heavy load had a lot of whipping motion as the mule walked down the trail.

As a rule, slings were used to pack long lengths of material. Long loads were packed lengthwise with the mule. The front of the load was lowered to allow a mule freedom for his head to maneuver around switchbacks in the trail and to prevent the animal from being hit by the whip-like motion of the load while traveling. The back of the load was raised to keep the load off their hips and to prevent rubbing. A diamond hitch was used to secure the load and a timber hitch placed on the ends of the load to take some of the whip out and to prevent the load from slipping ahead. Packer Foreman Bob McGregor designed wooden carriers in 1961 for the first packing of steel bridges. Slings would have put the load too high for these long, heavy lengths of steel. The carriers put the load closer to the mule's center of gravity, making the load ride better with less stress to the mule.

As equipment has gotten more complicated to pack, Packer Foreman Walt Castle has developed carriers, swivels, and frames to making packing of odd-ball material easier.

The Diamond Hitch, probably the oldest of all hitches in use today, is used primarily for top loads. By pulling the load into the animal, this hitch is harder on the pack animal than other types of hitches, but it keeps the higher toploads from shifting. Extra rope wrapped around each side of the load when the diamond is tied is called a "Yosemite wrap". A diamond hitch tied on the load with the woodstove is wrapped with what is called a "birdcage" to prevent the load from slipping ahead or back. There are many different ways to tie the diamond, depending on the packer tying it and what part of the country he comes from. Mules used to carry the stove and other high top loads have to be seasoned animals with good backs and be good travelers. Mules don't have as much wither as a horse and are rather round-backed. With a good stove-carrying mule, you could put a teacup of water on top of the load and never spill a drop. Not every packer had in his string a mule that would carry a stove. For instance in the late forties early fifties the NPS used primarily one mule named Stud for that purpose. The stove mule, regardless of the types of loads it carried, was always referred to as a stove mule. One mule was called Stover for his ability with stove loads.

Old style packing - 1928
load is bridge deck

Learning to tie the diamond is an on-the-job kind of thing. When Kenny Wass first came to work for the NPS in Yosemite, he said all he knew how to tie was the squaw hitch, and he had a lot of exciting times with top loads until he mastered the diamond. It did not take Kenny long to catch on because he was a good hand. Frank Coleman said, "The hitch all packers learn to tie first is the U Drag It Hitch. When you got tired of dragging it, you learned to pack it."

The box hitch is designed to pull the load away from the pack animal. Also called the squaw, basco, and sheepherder's hitch, lots of top loads have been packed with the box hitch, though it wasn't designed for such loads. When the load is riding right with the box hitch, the lash cinch will hang loose.

Sawbuck pack saddles have been used by the NPS throughout the packing history in Yosemite. Walt Castle in 1976 started to use a few Decker pack saddles along with the sawbucks. Raleigh (Sweet Pea) Patterson took an interest in the Decker and became very handy in its use. The Decker has an advantage over the sawbuck because the load is closer to the mule, and this makes it easier for the mule to carry. Pack bags are not needed, and a simple adjustment of the ropes makes it easier to adjust an unbalanced load.

The sawbucks is more functional on narrow, rocky Sierra trails because it allows the packer to build up more than out. The Decker is used more often in Rocky Mountain terrain where larger side loads are the rule. The Decker is used in Yosemite today primarily to pack the propane stoves and refrigerators for trail crew camps.

CCC Workers at Dirt Pit

National Park Service regulations now require pack stock to be tied together while traveling. If trail conditions are dangerous, pack stock can be turned loose until the bad section of trail is crossed. In the early years, pack stock were usually turned loose to travel, either herded along or between two or more packers. Pack stock travel better when loose because they can pick their own way along. The requirement to string mules together came with increased use in Yosemite's front- and back country.

In stringing mules together, the lead mule should be the one a packer is most likely to have a problem with – a young mule or a mule that is unsure of himself, for example. By leading this particular animal, the packer has better control of him should something go wrong. If a packer has two young mules in his string, the second one can be tied between two seasoned mules to help keep him in line. The last mule in the string is known as the "drag" or "whip" mule. He is selected for that spot for his traveling qualities because he has to keep up better around switchback corners or in rough terrain.

The old practice of belling the last mule in the string while traveling is required by NPS Packer Foreman Castle. The bell tells other parties on the trail that stock is coming up the trail. Some of the trails leading out of Yosemite Valley have only one or two places where stock can safely pass one another; hearing a bell, the packer nearest the passing spot can stop and wait for the other string to come along. The bell also tells a packer just how his mules are traveling and whether they are all hitched together. A packer should still look back at his string from time to time to see how the loads are riding. Some packers have been known to stuff their bells with newspaper or burlap. I guess the bell interrupted their sleep as they rode along.

Young mules have to be broken to pack. One, and not more than two unbroken mules can be worked in a string of seasoned animals. Loads on young mules should not be high and should not rattle. Seasoned mules are not all pets, but they are less likely to panic in a tight situation.

Bob McGregor would not start a mule until he was at least three years old. He said you work him and leave him alone. In the early years a lot of mules didn't get started until they were five or six years old. I can remember mules from a bucking string that were brought to Yosemite to be used as pack mules. These buggers never did get gentle, and they were packed until they were eighteen or twenty years old. They just got smarter and were less forgiving than a horse. After many seasons of use, it was still not uncommon to have to tie up a foot when saddling, packing, and unpacking these mules.

The Park Service had a mule through the '50's and early '60's that had been kept in a corral all winter and teased. Waine Westfall started this mule and worked him several seasons, but he never did get gentle. You couldn't blame the mule, because his first encounter with man hadn't been too pleasant. I had this mule in my string when he was about eighteen years old. Things were going along pretty well until I decided to pack a case of watermelons on him for a top load. The load rattled, and watermelons went out of there like cannonballs. I did the camp cook a favor because he didn't have to slice them when we got to the next camp site.

Dirt packing is not one of the most romantic jobs a packer can have, but it is a necessary part of trail building and maintenance. Sometimes dirt is shoveled into two piles and the mules are led between the piles. The packer with a helper shovels dirt into boxes that are hung on the mules, one man working on each side. The dirt boxes have a hinged bottom with a snap and hasp. When the packer reaches the site on the trail requiring the dirt, the hasp is tripped and the dirt falls out the bottom of the box.

A better system for obtaining dirt is a trench dug with dirt piled on each side. A string of mules is led into the trench, and trail workers load from each side while the packer uses his horse to hold the mules in line. These trenches or dirt pits are the best places to break stock to pack dirt because they can't jump out very easily.

Mules broken to pack dirt are the more seasoned ones. In 1957 the NPS began using Army mules mustered out of the U.S. Cavalry. Even though they were well broke, dirt packing was a new experience for them, and it took a while for them to get used to having dirt loaded and unloaded off them. Dirt pits were well away from the trail, found wherever good dirt was available.

When the job was finished, the pits were camouflaged. Early in the spring dirt was packed on all trails leading out of Yosemite Valley. When not packing supplies or moving camp, camp packers packed dirt on back country trails. Where drainage is not very good, dirt packing can be a waste of time. On the Merced Lake Trail above Twin Bridges, for example, dirt would be packed for two weeks on the trail only to be washed away in an afternoon thundershower. The raised trail treads or "causeways" built on that trail by Jim Snyder and crew in the '70's have a good drainage system, keeping the dirt covering in good shape today.

During Meyer's tenure furnishing stock for the Park Service a lot of the horses and mules weren't pets. One spring in the late fifties Horace sent a nice looking bay horse to the park that had bucked his son-in-law off and kicked him in the head. The horses name was Ally Oop, but after arriving at the park was renamed Snip. McGregor gave him to Walt Castle to ride. At the time Walt and Al Wass were cutting logs off of the trails in Wawona. Al said he heard a noise and looked back and all he could see was Castles boot tops above the Christmas trees. Snip was a treacherous ole bugger, strike or kick ya if he got the chance. I can vouch for the kicking part as he laid me up for a week and those were the days you didn't get paid when you couldn't work. Castle, after riding him all day had him tied to the ring by the tack room door where he unsaddle him, after putting his saddle up Walt stepped back outside and the ole horse jumped ahead as far as he could and tried to kick Castle. During a camp move to Wilmer Lake, Castle got in just before dark and that old horse stepped on a shovel, the handle hit him in the belly and he just swallowed his head and wadded up. Castle drove the iron in him and really put up a bronc ride. "Lost his hat tho". After Snip quit bucking Castle thought everybody wanted to see him get bucked off. "Shit" I never did like to see anybody hit the dirt and if I was ah horseback I'd do all I could to help a fella, run into his old horse or something. Of course sometimes you never had time it was over to quick.

I'll tell you one thing about old man Meyer if you couldn't ride one of his broncs he could, and make a hand on him to boot. George his son was the same way. "Hell in those early years I don't think they owned a gentle horse. Waine Westfall worked for Meyer in the mid-forties and said the last thing you thought of when you went to bed and the first thing you thought of when you got up was that old horse you had to ride. He told Meyer that a man sure must hated to walk to have have to want to ride these ole things.

There was a sorrel mare call the Pierson mare, cranky old thing, wad up and pitch every now and then. She bucked packer Joe Sebler off late in the fall of 1957. The river was low in the floor of Yosemite Valley and Joe was crossing it when she unloaded him in the cobble rocks. He sure lost a lot of hide on those rocks, a sorry sight when he came in that night. Walt Castle rode her a couple of seasons and she got better, kind of quit bucking, of course that's what everybody was working for, to help them get better.

Another horse that stands out in my mind was this roan horse of Meyers, coyote old bugger, hard to catch and kind of snakie. When you saddled him you best just throw the blankets and saddle on because if you tried to brush him he just might try and put one of those big number four hind shoes in your pocket. Because he was so hard to catch McGregor made a single hobble with about three feet of logging chain attached to it to put on his front pastern. The thought was that if he run off that he would bang his other leg with the log chain and stop. "Hell", he could go full out and never hit himself. In the mountains he would hide out, when you turned loose to graze. A little mule we called Jimmy took up with him, so we would bell them both. I've been on a ridge not a hundred yards away and watched those two walking along and neither one would ring those bells. You had to be as coyote as they were to catch them.

Some of the mules were kind of snakie too. The NPS had this ex-army mule, a big fella weighed about 1200 lbs., black with a lot of blue hair in his coat. His old neck was crooked where it had been pulled down and he had a strip of white hair on his poll just behind his ears were a chain had eaten into him at one time. A cinchie old bugger, when you saddle him in the barn in the morning you just hung the saddle on him and led him out to water, then took him on down to the hitch rail and chinch him up there. When you led him you better have him anchored to another horse or mule, because he had been spoiled and if you led him a foot he'd take off and ten men couldn't hold him. If you were careful when you cinched him up he wouldn't fall over backwards but he would always crow hop around. When he was led into the shoeing shop he got everybody's attention.

These are just a few stories of the many horses and mules that worked so hard, so a bunch of us could make a living.

These stories may sound like all the horses and mules were a bunch of broncs, but that wasn't the case. The majority of the stock were good usable animals, but in a herd the size of the NPS's you are bound to find a few head of stock that weren't to sure of themselves. The stock wasn't raised hand fed and alot of them were not started until they were five or six years old. The packers took pride in those horses and mules, and if one was a little rough to handle, they just did whatever it took to get the job done and tried to make them better.

Through the years, a lot of good men have worked for the NPS stables.

When I first went to work for the NPS in spring 1956, Alvis Brown, a Yosemite Indian born in El Portal, was the best packer I have ever seen, and that stands true today. Alvis could get along well with any kind of stock, and his packing abilities were second to none. One season he had a pretty rank mule in his string, and she was hard to catch as well. Packer Foreman Bob McGregor sent 30 feet of cotton rope out to Alvis so he could tie it in her halter and let her drag it when she was out to graze; this would make it easier to catch her when he wrangled in the mornings. Alvis just coiled the rope up and sent it back saying, "She won't learn anything with this on", and he got along just fine without it.

I asked Alvis how he learned to pack, and he always gave credit to Joe Rube and Louie Austin for helping him out. Both men were Native Americans raised at Bull Creek, Mariposa County. They had reputations of being top packers and are still talked about today by the few remaining people who knew and remember them. Alvis was just a kid about 16 years old when he, Austin, and Rube were packing from Harden Lake to Pate Valley. Being young he liked to sleep in. When he got up in the morning the mules would be caught and saddled. After breakfast Louie and Joe would pack up all the mules, and all Alvis had to do was lead them down the trail. Alvis said, "One morning I woke up, and everybody was gone. I had five mules and a whole lot of loads".

Bill Welch said that he and Alvis were going up country with loaded pack mules above Nevada Falls. Alvis was in the lead and riding a pretty snortie horse, and decided to eat his lunch. His lunch was in a paper bag and when Alvis reached for his sandwich, the bag rattled, the Indian went one way, the horse the other. When Alvis got back on he said he didn't think he would eat his lunch on him anymore.

Alvis Brown - 1954

At the end of a season years ago Alvis and I were in the town of Mariposa at the local watering hole. Alvis came along and said, "I got two womans, Bob. You want one?" I said, "No, not now, Alvis; maybe later".

Alvis was proud of the fact that he was a packer. Sometimes after partaking of the spirits, he would say, "I'm Alvis Brown, number one United States Government Packer, brother in law". Sometimes it would be "cousin". When Alvis left the park in 1957 he was the last of the old-time packers who had packed in Yosemite during the '20's. Alvis was a good friend and fellow worker.

I miss him.

The early day packer grew up around stock, Frank Coleman a local Miwok Indian was one of them. Born and raised around Coulterville, California, Frank started driving teams of horses and mules, hauling freight to Yosemite and later drove stage coach. He packed for the Coffman Kinny Co., in Yosemite as well as for many commercial packers. In 1916 he worked as a teamster for the NPS in Yosemite. When the building of the Hetch Hetchy reservoir started Frank drove a chain driven Rio truck from the gravel pit near Miguel Meadow, down the grade to the dam site. In 1956 Frank again returned to Yosemite to pack for the NPS, that season Frank was the packer that went from camp to camp helping the camp packer move the trail camps.

Coleman was a big man he weighed I guess close to 300 lbs., Bob McGregor issued Frank a big horse weighing close to 1500 lbs. and Frank despite his size never hurt a horses back. In his younger years men that remembered him said he could lift a 50 gallon drum of fuel into the bed of a pick-up. Cement is often needed for backcountry work, bridge abutments and so forth, when the truck with cement arrived to the packing area Frank would put a 94 lb. sack under each arm and walk across the yard with it.

Frank after a days work would clean up and he always buttoned his collar button of his shirt, he shined like a new dollar. My mother said he was the most immaculate man she ever saw.

1957 Frank decided not to pack anymore and he drove the grocery truck and trail tractor for trail supervisor Doug Thomas. Packers referred to the truck as the candy wagon. Frank was as handy with equipment as he was stock. He had the ability of being able to watch something being done, then he could go do it himself.

For a couple of years he batched in camp 6 with Walt Castle and myself and the bears bothered him, he would go to the shower about 10 o'clock at night and I can still hear him hollering all the way over and back. Walt and I started calling him Teddy.

Frank Coleman and Walt Castle - 1950's

The last time I saw Frank on the trail he was packing for Joe Barns out of Mather, Frank was in his 70's. I ran into him where the Jack Main trail leaves the Lake Elenore road a place called Tin Shack. He said that he had been down to Art Vancores Saddle Shop and wanted a new saddle. Art told him it would be two years before he could get one. Frank said hell I need it now when you get up to my age you never know when the lights are going out. When Frank decided to quit the mountains he settled down on his home at Chicken Ranch RD., below Jamestown, Ca., and could often be seen driving the stage coach at Columbia State Park. Frank passed away in 1973.

Bill Welch early day Yosemite packer and life long cattleman was raised in La Grange, California on the Hayward Ranch. This ranch was the headquarters for the Tim Carlon ranches. Bill is a stepson to Carlon, so he was introduced to the stock business early in life. As a young boy he started working with the cattle and horses and at the age of ten went to work as a guide for the Yosemite Park & Curry Co. at their stables in Yosemite Valley. Jim Helm was the stable boss at that time. Helm also owned a ranch in White Rock (Mariposa Co.) were Curry wintered their horses and mules. Through the years Bill worked on and off for the Curry Co and during his tenure with the Company worked under all of the old stable managers. The first being Helm, then Jim Barnett, Jess Rust and finally Bob Barnett. Some of the local people that Bill worked with during those early years were George Barnett, Malcolm Fulmer, Evert Phelp, Al Kay and Berthia Blanchett.

Bill packed for the NPS stables in 1927 to 1928 and from 1931 to 1938. At that time Joe Gabarnio Head Teamster was in charge of the NPS stables.

A lifetime of working with livestock and good hands contributed to the fact that Bill himself is an exceptional good hand, quiet and takes good care of his stock.

During the early fifties (1951-1954) Bill operated a stable at White Wolf within Yosemite. This stable provided pack trips and day rides for the tourist. In the fall of the year he would drive about forty head of horses and mules from

Bill Welch

there to Kennedy Meadows and would throw in with Frank Kursies pack outfit and pack deer hunters. The route Bill took on this drive went through Pate Valley to Pleasant Valley, Kerrick Canyon via Bear Valley, Stubblefield Canyon, Wilmer Lake over Bond Pass and finally Kennedy, a drive that took three days.

While operating the stable at White Wolf, Bill opened a stable at Mather, located near the park boundary. This stable was known as the 4 Bar stable and he operated it until the early sixties. By then Bill had his cattle herd built up to where it required all of his time, so he closed the stable.

Today Bill still runs a few cattle and lives with his wife Helen in La Grange California.

Charlie Gilmore only packed for the NPS in Yosemite one season, that was in 1957. Charlie was about 32 years old at the time but he brought a vast knowledge and experience with him. He was raised on California's east side around Lone Pine and started packing at the age of ten. Following those early years he came to Yosemite, packed for the Park & Curry Co. for several years.

He was an exceptional mule man, quite around stock. When Charlie was mad or upset the only way you could tell was that he referred to the mules as burros.

Charlie Gilmore - 1957

The season Charlie worked for the NPS he was a camp packer for a trail crew. Charlie took a lot of pride in his work, he built eight drift fences and gates in Yosemite's north end. The gates were of pole construction with augured holes for the cross poles. The gate hinges were made from a forked limb and the gate swung from a flat rock placed at the bottom of the main gate pole. Today after 30 years only one of these gates remain, its found at the lower end of Pate Valley. Charlie passed away several years ago.

Charlies Gate at
Pate Valley

The Alberta boys were of the younger generation of NPS packers in Yosemite. Mike, Coleman and Jeff (Lug Bolt) worked at the NPS stables during the seventies. All were experienced horsemen that had grown up on a ranch. Because of their ranch background they could run equipment as well as cowboy.

Their father Joe was a well known horseman and stock raiser, so these young men grew up working and the cowboy instilled in them at an early age. Johnny Jones their uncle ran a pack station for years out of Globe Rock near Jackass Meadows and is a legend among packers today. With Joe and Johnny's help they had no choice except to be handy around stock.

Today Coleman trains horses on his ranch near Coursegold California, Luggie has a logging business and Mike lives near Raymond, California, shoes horses and is in the cattle business.

The old time packer grew up around stock. Those with ranch experience were cowboys to start with. They already had the horse part and had only to learn the packing, if they didn't already know. Old hands would take a young fellow starting out and help him learn when they were in the back country.

They would never show you anything in front of anybody, because they didn't want to show people how little you knew. That was the old way. Today's generation of young people interested in packing as a rule don't have the stock handling background. They not only have to learn the packing skills but the horse skills as well. The interested ones make good hands, and the NPS is fortunate to have some of these young packers working for them today.

But there are not many old hands left working for the Park Service to pass on the skills of the trade.

Bill Welch leading tour group
Yosemite Valley - 1920's

Chapter 11

TRAIL SIGNS

Cavalry T Blaze

When Anglos first entered Yosemite's back country, trails the Indians had followed were unmarked. Some of the first marks or blazes made on trees to mark the way were simple axe marks or chips cut in the outer bark. Many of these remaining blazes were made by sheepmen, cattlemen, or miners after 1850. The U.S. Cavalry and the sheepmen often carved on trees, leaving initials, dates, or a drawing.

In 1894, as the Cavalry started to push the outer borders of Yosemite's back country in search of poachers and stockmen, main trail routes became established. The standard "T" blaze the Cavalry used can be seen today along most major trail routes. Cavalry troopers joked that they used "T" for "trail" so the Irish troopers could find their way home. "Monuments" of small rocks were another method of marking a trail, and similar "rock ducks" or cairns are still used often on cross-country routes.

By 1917 the NPS started to use the diamond blaze to mark trails, and by 1926 enamel regulation signs were nailed to trees to mark the way and define location. These signs were put up by back country rangers. By 1931 these enamel signs were on all bridle paths on the floor of Yosemite Valley.

In 1935 the NPS purchased a Roover Press that made small signs embossed on aluminum. Civilian Conservation Corps workers made the signs, and NPS rangers nailed them to trees by the trail and in established campsites.

In 1941 redwood signs were introduced to the trail system. These signs were packed in by mule to all trail junctions, passes, lakes, and campsites.

The signs were bolted on posts cut on site, then planted in the ground. The letters on these signs were routed in the wood and painted white. Bears took a liking to this new redwood sign and would manicure their teeth and nails on them. This damage meant constant replacement. In 1951 Jeffrey Pine was used on an experimental basis to find a type of wood that might not attract old teddy, but the results were the same.

Bill Kirk, a long time NPS employee in the welding shop, was instructed in 1952 to build metal signs on a trial basis. The letters were stencilled on the metal, then Bill cut out the letters freehand with a cutting torch.

Bears didn't bother these signs on iron posts, and these signs mark all NPS trails today. Bill Kirk's artistic design and care with individual letters can be distinguished from those signs made today because he was a highly skilled artist with metals, welding, and the torch.

NPS packer Merle Williams, along with a helper, packed and put up all of the metal signs in Yosemite's south end in 1955. In 1957 sawyer Joe Akerson and I packed and put up all of the metal signs in Yosemite's north end. The sign posts were five feet in length and had to be slung on the sides of the mules. All material was packed out of Tuolumne Meadows to Virginia Canyon, a round trip of 26 miles, a job which took several days and trips to complete.

After all signs and posts were stashed in Virginia Canyon, a base camp was set up in the canyon and signs were dispersed from there. When signs were placed at all passes, junctions, lakes, and canyons from there to the Smedberg Lake-Rodgers Canyon area, the rest of the material was packed from Virginia Canyon to Benson Lake. A base camp was set up at Benson and the remaining signs in the north end were put up from that camp.

The wooden signs had one distinct advantage over any other type of sign: the white lettering made them easier to see at night. Back country rangers like Clyde Quick always carried a brush and small can of white paint to touch up the letters on signs. Clyde also knew to put a flat rock in the hole under the post to prevent snow from pushing the sign into the ground. With iron posts, workers often drove the post into the ground without this precaution, and signs got lower to the ground each year.

Chapter 12

WOMEN PACKERS

Johanna Wheeler Gehres

Johanna Wheeler Gehres was the first woman to pack for the NPS Stables. Johanna was born and raised in Yosemite Valley. At fourteen she went to work as a guide for the Yosemite Park and Curry Company Stables. During the time she worked at the Curry Stables, she advanced from guide to packer.

She attended Merced College in the fall of 1984, enrolled in the colt training class, and took other horse management classes. The spring of 1985 found her taking the horseshoeing class. By the end of the school year, Johanna received the Horse Management award for excellence.

In summer 1985, Johanna went to work at the NPS Stables. She packed for Jim Snyder's trail camp, proving herself a very capable hand who got along with stock and was able to shoe her own stock when the need arose. In 1986 and 1987 she packed again for the Curry Stables. She returned to the NPS Stables in 1988 to work as a packer, cleaning the barn, feeding the stock, helping packers to pack up, shoeing horses and mules when needed, and riding some of the young colts. Packer Foreman Walt Castle gives high praise for the job Johanna performs at the stables.

In 1987 Debbie Dalee was hired to pack for Resources Management in Tuolumne Meadows. She also helped pack to the Vogelsang High Sierra Camp sewer mound project. Debbie's eyes got pretty big one day when lightning approached her mule-loads of explosives, so quickly she had to unpack and wait out the storm.

Debbie Dalee

Debbie was born in Colorado and came out to California at the age of seventeen, working one season as a guide at the Curry Stables. She also attended Merced College, where she took horse management classes and received the Horse Management award. She completed law enforcement training at Santa Rosa, California. During 1988 she worked as a jailer for NPS, but, because of her expertise with horses, she could be found on her days off with the NPS horse patrol.

Virginia Gilmore never packed for the NPS but she was capable of it and deserves mention. She and her husband Charlie came to work for the NPS in Yosemite spring of 1957. Virginia cooked for Rockey Cameans trail crew and Charlie was the camp packer. She was handy with stock and an excellent cook. Her previous experience around stock and camp cooking were the years she cooked for the Sierra Club on their annual trips through the Sierras. These trips saw them bring over 100 head of stock through the mountains. It was while on one of these trips she met Charlie.

The trail crew was camped at Neil Meadow and one afternoon while the crew was out working on the trail, two young backcountry rangers rode into camp, Virginia invited them for lunch. Turning their stock out to graze while they dined they soon found out after they had eaten that they couldn't catch the stock. Virginia watched for a while, then quietly went out and caught up their horses.

Virginia Gilmore

Tony DeBellis' trail crew worker at the time said the thing he remembers most about Virginia was that she was always pleasant and that she could do any chore around camp with ease. Virginia now lives in Arizona.

Chapter 13

Tenaya Lake Lodge - High Sierra Camp - 1928

HIGH SIERRA CAMPS

The Desmond Park Company built the first back country camp at Merced Lake in 1916. After 1919 several camps were added to provide hikers with meals and overnight facilities in the back country. These early camps consisted of a mess tent and separate sleeping tents for men and women. The camps had primitive toilet facilities, simple pit toilets of the one- and two-hole type, providing a choice if you wanted company or not when nature called. Sites of the first camps were Merced Lake, Boothe Lake, and two roadside camps at Tenaya Lake and Tuolumne Meadows.

The Boothe Lake camp was moved after a few years to the trail junction of Vogelsang, Rafferty Creek, and the Lyell Fork. In 1940 this camp was moved again to its present location on Fletcher Creek where it is known as the Vogelsang High Sierra Camp. In 1927 the Glen Aulin camp was established. In 1938 the Tenaya Lake camp was moved to May Lake, where it is still in use.

The Sunrise High Sierra Camp was constructed in Long Meadow in 1960. Construction started in June and was completed by mid-October. Steve Wight and myself packed for the plumbing crew constructing sewer and water facilities for this new camp. Claude Cottrell was the plumber supervisor; John Banias was foreman on the job site; and Bill Hook was the camp cook.

When the plumbers went into the back country, they went in style with hot running water and showers. We put up a small corral by the road camp in Tuolumne Meadows, today's visitor center, and all packing was done from there. A total of 18 miles round trip was made daily. The camp at Sunrise was supplied weekly, as all camps on these projects were.

To get the heavier equipment, such as stove parts, in for the new camp, Curry Company packers Vern "Mogue" Morris and Bill Butler used an aparejo pack saddle. Common among cavalry packers in the 1890's, this type of saddle was replaced by the sawbucks by the First World War. Packing for the Sunrise Camp was the last time an aparejo was used in Yosemite.

While the concessionaire built and maintained these camps, the National Park Service provided and maintained water and sewer facilities for each camp. As increasing use put greater demands on the camps, they were enlarged, and more modern facilities were installed. Today these camps have flush toilets, showers, and some chemical toilets are used as well. As use has increased, water and sewer facilities have been enlarged to meet the demands of each camp. Because these camps are miles by trail from the roads, most material for these projects has been packed in on mules. Water quality at the camps is closely monitored by Park Service employees with the assistance of Curry Company employees as well.

In 1984 the Glen Aulin camp sewer system was enlarged and modernized with a new mound-type leach field. This was the first work to be done on this camp's sewer system since 1962. Dan Jones and Billy Fouts packed in a construction camp. Lumber and pipe in 8- and 10-foot lengths along with cement and equipment were packed in daily from Tuolumne Meadows. Cement mixers, wheelbarrows, jackhammers, generators, and all kinds of hand tools went in to Glen Aulin by mule. After digging and blasting a hole for the new septic tank, crew members broke up rock from the pit to gravel size with sledge hammers for use in the leach field. A team of mules pulling a Fresno scraper brought in dirt to cover the leach field.

In 1985 the septic system at Merced Lake was overhauled and enlarged by Park Service workers and a California Conservation Corps crew. Billy Fouts, Sweet Pea, Steve Ybarra, Jamie Watts, Craig Ritchie, and Dan Jones packed on this project which was started in late May and completed by July. In fall 1985, Steve Ybarra, Johanna (Wheeler) Gehres, Billy Foutes, and Dan Jones began packing for the May Lake system. Fall snow brought the packing to a close as workers saw trenches fill with snow faster than they could dig them out. The project was completed the following year when Dan Jones, John Moe, and Billy Fouts packed material in.

The Vogelsang septic system was overhauled in 1987, a job that lasted four and a half months. Mark Messenger, David Dye, and myself packed for this project. The dry year made it possible for packing to get under way the second week of June, and we were packing into mid-October. Because of the shortage of rock near the job site, 90 yards of pumice was packed in for the leach field. With the closing down of trail camps in the fall, all the Park Service packers went to work packing on this job, including Billy Fouts, Leonard Domingues, John Moe, Kermit Radoor, Sweet Pea, Dan Kirn, and Debbie Dalee.

Packing for the Vogelsang project was done out of Tuolumne Meadows. Packers made a 15-mile round trip daily, double-tripping the distance on occasion. A CCC construction camp was set up a quarter mile west of the job site. Packers supplied the camp twice a week with fresh supplies. Toward the end of the season high winds blew the camp tents down and it took a full day to rebuild the camp. Because of the scarcity of dirt in the rocky terrain, dirt to cover the leach field had to be packed on mules. Along with the every day packing of cement, pipe, and lumber, 20-foot lengths of 4-inch plastic pipe were packed on two mules with a swivel invented by Walt Castle. Ten pieces of pipe were packed at a time, and the swivel enabled the mules to make turns at each switchback in the trail.

Because of the 1987 drought, mules packed water from Tuolumne Meadows to Sunrise from late August until the closing of the camp. Two strings of mules twice a week were required to supply the camp's needs. In 1988 a new and larger water system was developed for Sunrise, and hopefully it will fill the camp's needs for years to come.

The trail connecting the high sierra camps is known as the High Sierra Loop trail. Because of the influx of people during the peak summer season, a ranger station is maintained in Little Yosemite Valley. Rangers work foot patrol out of this camp and live in tent quarters. Pack mules supply the camp. Chemical toilets are available for visitors and are maintained by the National Park Service. One packer working daily out of Yosemite Valley makes a trip to Little Yosemite, cleans the toilets, and packs the human waste out.

The sewer and water facilities at the high camps require constant maintenance. Men and mules have to do the job, and, as long as these camps remain, mules will have a job to do.

Bertha Blancett

Indian Field Days - 1920's

Indian Field Days Rough & Tumble Potato Race

Chapter 14

The Original Rangers - 1916

MOUNTED HORSE PATROL & BACK COUNTRY RANGERS

From 1915 to the early 1950's mounted rangers were a visible part of Yosemite's front- and back country. The early day back country rangers were made up mostly of seasonal help, and the men who held these positions were generally from the surrounding counties. These men were experienced horsemen with ranch and stock background. Working seasonally for the Park Service was a way to supplement their income not far from home. Some of the early rangers were Arch Westfall, Charlie Adair, Waine E. Westfall, Jack Gaylor, Archie Leonard, Henry Skelton, and Billy Nelson. These men knew stock and the mountains.

Often traveling cross-country because trails were rough or incomplete, early rangers patrolled park boundaries very often to keep a watchful eye for livestock or hunters entering the park. A ranger traveled with his horse and pack animal, returning to the front country only for fresh supplies. Some early patrol stations were Hog Ranch (Mather), Tuolumne Meadows, Crane Flat, Benson Lake, and Deer Camp. Front country patrols worked out of Yosemite Valley and Wawona. The majority of back country rangers work alone, and for the most part, their job is for an individual who doesn't mind spending long periods of time alone in the back country.

Old time back country rangers depended on their skills and experience, entering the back country when the first snow melted and leaving when the snow flew again in the fall.

Deer Camp ranger patrol cabin was built in 1916, allowing rangers easy access to Yosemite's southern back country. In 1930 a ranger patrol cabin was built in the south end of the park at Buck Camp. Today the Deer Camp patrol cabin is gone, but back country rangers are stationed during the summer and fall at Buck Camp. Early rangers camped at Tuolumne Meadows as a base camp to patrol much of Yosemite's north end. In 1924 a ranger station was built at Tuolumne Meadows, which remains a base for both front- and back country rangers. A ranger patrol cabin was built at Merced Lake in 1926 by the Merced Irrigation District for winter snow surveys.

Herb Ewing went to work for the NPS road crew in 1946. After six months on the road crew, Herb transferred to the ranger force. From 1951 to 1955 Herb was the back country ranger at Merced Lake. Herb's wife Ruth and son Bobbie stayed at the lake with Herb during his tenure as a back country ranger. Growing up in Yosemite Valley, Herb knew the back country well; he and Ruth were both expert fishermen. In 1956 Herb was appointed District Ranger at Tuolumne Meadows. He continued to oversee much of the back country in his district and took several back country trips annually. Herb retired in 1977 and lives with Ruth at Pine Mountain Lake near Groveland, where they can see Mt. Conness from their back porch.

Glen Fredy - Back Country Ranger

Jerry Mernin came to Yosemite as a seasonal back country ranger in 1958. Jerry had just graduated from law school and was stationed at Merced Lake for his first job as a ranger. Packers referred to him as "the Philadelphia lawyer". As a back country ranger he wore out a lot of horse and mule shoes traveling over the country; he didn't let much grass grow under his feet. With horse manure on him and his love for the outdoors, he gave up a career in law and received a permanent ranger job in Yellowstone National Park. He has remained there throughout his career and is currently a District Ranger, riding the back country trails every chance he gets.

Glen Fredy is a back country ranger who has worked for the National Park Service for 19 seasons. Glen works out of Tuolumne Meadows and patrols Yosemite's north end. He is capable of shoeing his own stock, is a good hand with a horse, and can handle a full string of mules if the need arises. His back country experience and knowledge make him a valuable asset to the NPS ranger force.

Clyde Quick grew up on a ranch in Ben Hur, (Mariposa County) and worked as a seasonal back country ranger in Yosemite from 1944 to 1973. Clyde being raised on a ranch and around stock, understood that a cow couldn't read boundary signs. So any cattle that strayed onto park land was no big deal to him. If the owner couldn't be contacted Clyde simple moved the cattle himself.

Jimmy Lee, law enforcement ranger in Yosemite during the 1970's and mid 1980's, was a back country ranger 1979 and 1980 seasons. Jimmy attended Castle's horse training session and Walt said of Jimmy, that he had that natural ability around stock that he should have been a horse trainer. Jimmy was a hard worker and well liked by everyone. He said his fondest years as a ranger were those spent as a back country ranger.

One of the highlights for early mounted rangers was their participation in the Indian Field Days held in Yosemite Valley during the '20's. Indian ladies exhibited and sold baskets while cowboys, rangers, and Indians from Yosemite and the east side competed in the potato race, trick riding and roping, horse racing, and bronc riding. Harry Tom, a Piute man from Mono Lake with a reputation as an outstanding horseman, competed at these field days. Bob McGregor said Harry was one you always had to beat in the horse race. Bob said, "Competitors hemmed Harry up in one preliminary race, but his horses were too good, and Harry was too smart, and in the final race he beat everybody." There was always friendly rivalry between the competitors.

Pooch Brown, speaking about riding bucking horses, said, "Harry rides with a tight rein; when I ride, I pitch 'em the slack." Nonetheless, they were both top riders.

My grandfather, Waine E. Westfall, was an early day back country ranger. He wanted to play with the rangers in the Potato Race at one of the last Indian Field Days. Since he was no longer employed by the NPS at the time, the rangers wouldn't let him play on their side. He played with the Indians instead, and they beat the tail off the rangers.

Today back country rangers are stationed at Buck Camp, Tuolumne Meadows, Merced Lake, and Miguel Meadows. Rangers also work from Hetch Hetchy and Harden Lake. Front country mounted rangers are stationed in Yosemite Valley, Wawona, and Tuolumne Meadows.

After a number of years without front country mounted rangers, the horse patrol was revived in 1966 for two seasons. After the July 1970 riots, the horse patrol was brought back to Yosemite with ten rangers employed. The first ranger in charge of the horse patrol was Pete Thompson. Walt Castle, Packer Foreman, attended four week-long police horse seminars in Washington D.C. The Park Service purchased horses, all sorrel in color and of uniform height and weight. Castle started these horses in training to meet the needs and requirements of a patrol horse. These horses have to be unafraid of noises, crowds, and unfamiliar objects as well as being responsive to the rider's commands. Because most present day rangers do not have horse experience and the Park Service does not require it in hiring rangers, a horse training school for park rangers was established in 1976. The six week school was taught by Walt Castle, with rangers attending from parks all over the western states as well as from Yosemite. It is because of this school the mounted rangers of Yosemite are of the highest calibar. Because of Walt's workload,

Horse Patrol - Class of 1985

ranger Dan Horner, assisted by Colin Campbell, taught the school in 1988.

Since 1970, other park rangers who have been in charge of the horse patrol have been Paul Henry, Charlie (Butch) Wilson, and Ron Mackie.

Tim McMillen, no longer with the NPS, was a long time front country patrol ranger and was an outstanding horseman who was capable of shoeing his own horse and on his days off would often help the horseshoer. Tim often rode a lot of the young horses for Walt while on patrol.

Today Maynard Medefind, who has just completed 20 seasons as a seasonal ranger, has been with the Horse Patrol from the start. Maynard works out of Tuolumne Meadows and is an excellent horseman. He also rides a lot of the young patrol horses for Castle.

Ron Mackie started his career with the National Park Service in Yosemite in 1960. He worked the summer season on trail crews and attended college in the fall and winter. Ron worked on Bob Barr's trail crew from 1960 to June 1965, starting out as an axeman and working his way up to Foreman I.

Working on Barr's trail crew for that many seasons says a lot about Mackie. Barr ran one of the hardest working crews in the back country. One season Barr went through three complete crews in six weeks while camped at City Camp before he found a crew that was tough enough to do the work he expected. He had one crew working, one walking out, and another walking in. Mackie said Barr would be down the trail laying riprap or rolling rocks out of the trail but looking back between his legs to see if the crew was working.

With his trail crew background, Ron became back country ranger at Buck Camp in July 1965. In 1966 he worked the mounted horse patrol and in 1967 was stationed at Mather. While at Mather he received a permanent appointment. He attended the Horace Albright Training

Waine E. Westfall, author's grandfather - 1916

Center and graduated December 1967. With the exception of one year as a ranger in Yellowstone, Ron has been with the NPS in Yosemite. In 1975 he was appointed Wilderness Manager, a position he holds today. People often wonder why Mackie is so hard to get hold of, but he is out in the field doing the job he was hired for. With his trail crew, horse, and back country background, the Park Service could not ask for a better Wilderness Manager.

Jimmy Lee
Back Country Ranger

Ron Mackie
Wilderness Manager

Chapter 15

Bob McGregor and Kenny Wass load High Camp outhouse - 1967

TITLES AND PAY

In 1915 the rate of pay for a government packer was $3 per day. By 1929 pay for that position had increased to $5 per day. At the beginning of the Depression in 1930 pay was reduced to $4.50 a day. Four packers were selected as senior packers between 1931 and 1935; pay for that position was $4.75 per day, two bits a day more than for a packer. In July 1935, the pay for all National Park Service employees changed to pay by the hour. Packers were paid $.56 an hour. In 1971 the title of packer changed to Animal Packer, and in 1976 a job description for a packer trainee was established, and the position was called horse-handler. Until 1960 seasonal workers did not earn sick leave or annual leave. If you missed a day's work, you missed a day's pay, holidays included.

Until 1975 packers and trail crews worked six days a week. The six-day week took advantage of the fact that most camps were too far back for crews to come out on weekends. The extra work day meant more got done over the short high country work season. While the six-day week cost more, production on the trail was also much higher than a five-day work week. It is difficult to work five days a week in the back country and accomplish very much.

The rate of pay in 1915 for a teamster was $3 per day, increasing by 1925 to 4.75 a day. This was the last year teamsters were used in large numbers, because motor vehicles were replacing horse drawn equipment in Yosemite, though a few teamsters were used until 1932.

In 1915 the blacksmith received $3 per day. In 1959, the last year this job title was used, the rate of pay was $2.29 an hour. The head blacksmith was also the horseshoer, though in 1918, 1925, and 1930 to 1932, several men were hired specifically to shoe horses. These men worked under the head blacksmith. In 1959 a permanent position of horseshoer was created, but it was called "packer". This permanent position was phased out in 1983, and horseshoeing is now done by seasonal employees.

Until the late 1950's checks were handed out in front of the timekeeper's office. If a worker wasn't on hand to pick up his check, it was held for him at the ranger's headquarters in Government Center, where a ranger was on duty at the front desk twenty-four hours a day.

Hiring and firing were much simpler thirty years ago. You just showed up at the barn. If you were hired, you were sent over to the personnel office, filled out a couple of papers, raised your hand and took the oath, and went to work. The bull cook in Camp 1 issued you blankets for which you were charged $.35 a night. You ate in the mess hall at Camp 1 for $1.05 a meal.

A register was started in 1959, and everybody who wanted to work as a packer had to fill out the paperwork to get on the register. In 1960 the highest scoring man on the packers' register came to work in Yosemite. He couldn't lead a horse out of the barn and couldn't pack his lunch, but I guess he knew how to fill out papers. Once you were hired and came back every year you didn't have to do any more paperwork.

Today you have to fill out application forms every year and compete for a job. On top of that, once you receive notice that you're hired, you fill out more forms that ask you the same questions that you filled out on your original application. Some of the forms you have to get notarized, and, by the time you're through, the stack of paper is as big as the Sears Roebuck catalog. Computers and bureaucracy have made it damn near like some college graduate writing a thesis for his doctorate just to get hired. Then, after working for them a lot of years, you still have to prove you're a United States citizen and have a Social Security card. Somebody has educated themselves beyond their intelligence. Hiring has become a literacy test in which neither mountain nor horse-sense plays any role.

Chapter 16

Leonard Domingues

EMPLOYEES AND TITLES

The following pages present a list of the packers, teamsters, and horseshoers who have worked at the National Park Service Stables since 1915.

Through the years the local Indians have contributed a major part of this labor force, dedicating themselves to the job at hand and always giving their best. To recognize these people, I have put "N.A." for Native American by each of their names. Through the history of the National Park Service in Yosemite, Indian people have not only worked at the stables but in all areas of park maintenance and forestry. Today there are two young men at the NPS Stables carrying on a tradition that is much a part of their heritage.

Leonard Domingues was born and raised in Yosemite Valley and works as an NPS packer. He got his start as a packer working at the Curry Stables, starting as a guide and working up to packer. He attended Merced College horseshoeing school and went to work at the NPS Stables in 1983. Leonard started as a horsehandler and is now a packer who has proven himself a capable hand.

Paco Harlow is the NPS horseshoer. He was raised in Raymond in Madera County. His father, Ernie, has shod horses for over 40 years. Paco learned the craft well from him. Paco has been with the Park Service in Yosemite since 1986.

HORSESHOERS AND BLACKSMITHS

1. H. Argall — 1925
2. J.B. Ashworth — 1924
3. Hugh Babcock — 1936, 1938, 1948, 1951
4. Joe Barnes — 1930, 1931
5. Bob Barrett — 1964, 1965, 1979
6. Fredrick Bruschi — 1916-1920, 1924-1926, 28, 30
7. Walt Castle Jr. — 1965-1969
8. John Dunn — 1916
9. J. Coster — 1919-1920
10. Jamie Egan — 1924
11. Roy Ernst — 1923
12. D.E. Evans — 1932
13. Emmett Field — 1922, 1923
14. John Franco — 1930
15. D.S. Gallison — 1916
16. Dan Garvey — 1925
17. Eddie Gordon — 1930
18. W.J. Hagan — 1919
19. Jerry (Paco) Harlow — 1986-1988 (N.A.)
20. Chas. Harris — 1918
21. Frank Hendricks — 1918
22. Frank Hiniker — 1933
23. John Hanks — 1918
24. W.J. Hogge — 1916, 1917
26. E.C. Hunt — 1919
27. Andy Lane — 1916
28. J.H. Johnston — 1931
29. M.L. Jordan — 1916
30. A. Maxwell — 1917
31. D.A. Miller — 1916
32. Wm. McDaniel — 1931
33. Robt. O'Herin — 1916
34. Thomas Owen — 1938
35. Frank Oyler — 1938 (N.A.)
36. J. Hinken — 1916, 1917
37. John Peters — 1931, 1932
38. T. Ryan — 1925
39. Theodore Sidor — 1947
40. Frank Vanciel — 1932
41. J.T. Ward — 1934-1935
42. Rick Watson — 1972-1980
43. Michel Weinberg — 1920
44. Waine Westfall — 1952, 1956-1963
45. Clair Wolfsen — 1950, 1952-1956

N. P. S. PACKERS
(1915-1988)

1. Coleman Alberta — Packer 1975 to 1978
2. Jeff Alberta — Packer 1971 to 1973
3. Mike Alberta — Packer 1971 to 1973
4. David Apako — Packer 1984
5. Harvey Arancibia — Packer 1956, 57, 60, 62
6. George Ashworth — Packer 1942 to 1946
7. Tyrone Atwater — Packer 1983
8. J.B. Austin — Packer 1960
9. Louie Austin (N.A.) — Sr. Packer 1918-1923, 1935 to 1949
10. Joe Barnes — Packer 1933
    Joe Barnes — Horseshoer 1930, 1931
11. Robert L. Barrett — Packer 1962
12. Robert (Bob) Barrett — Packer 1956 to 1965, 1986 to 1988
    Robert (Bob) Barrett — Horseshoer 1964 to 1965, 1979
13. Harry Bartlett — Packer 1951 to 1952
14. Sidney Bridges — Packer 1970
15. Alvis Brown (N.A.) — Packer 1925 to 1957
16. Mike Brown — Packer 1977 to 1983
17. Charlie Brous — Packer 1956 to 1957
18. Walt Butler — Packer 1972 to 1974
19. Wes Burdick — Packer 1950
20. George Calkins — Packer 1942 to 1954
21. D.R. Carlon — Packer 1924
22. Richard Carr — Packer 1983
23. Walt Castle — Packer 1957 to 1960, 1962
    Walt Castle — Horseshoer 1965 to 1969
    Walt Castle Jr. — Packer Foreman 1970-1988
24. Phil Chapman — Packer 1962
25. Max Cheshier — Packer 1959 to 1967
26. Hyde Clark — Corralman 1917 to 1918
    Hyde Clark — Herder 1917
27. John Coclazer — Packer 1973 to 1974
28. Frank Coleman (N.A.) — Packer 1956
    Frank Coleman (N.A.) — Teamster 1916 to 1918,
29. Garland Compton — Horsehandler 1976
30. Edmund Coyle — Packer 1915
31. Martin Culp — Packer 1919 to 1921, 23, 24
32. Debbie Dalee — Packer 1987
33. Bill Dayton — Packer 1951
34. Ralph DeGraff — Packer 1946
35. Joseph DellOrto — Packer 1976
36. Evert DeMoss — Packer 1950, 51, 53, 54, 55, 57
37. L. Domingues (N.A.) — Packer 1985 to 1988
    L. Domingues (N.A.) — Horsehandler '83 to '84
38. Dennis Dozier — Packer 1988
39. John Drayer — Packer 1941
40. David Dye — Packer 1987 to 1988
41. Eric Erickson — Packer 1967 to 1973
42. Roy Ernst — Packer 1923
43. Lawrence Flournoy — Packer 1980
44. Wm. (Bill) Fouts — Packer 1982 to 1988
45. Diovannie J. Franco — Packer 32 to 36, 38, 39
46. John Franco — Packer 1935

47. Dan Fraser	Packer 1981 to 1985	77. Albert Knapp	Packer 1951
48. James Fulmer	Packer 1942	78. John Lawrence (N.A.)	Packer 1915
49. Joe Gaberino	Head Teamster 1916 to 1938	79. Gerald Leonard (N.A.)	Packer 1963 to 1965
50. Bill Gann	Packer 1950 to 1952	80. Jim Leonard	Packer 1970
51. Leon Garcia	Packer 1974 to 1985	81. W.P. Lock	Packer 1919
52. Dan Garvey	Horseshoer 1925	82. Ed Mankins	Packer 1960
53. Johanna (Wheeler) Gehres	Packer 85 to 88	83. Joe S. Marks	Packer 1935 to 1936
54. Charlie Gilmore	Packer 1957	84. Kerry Maxwell	Packer 1969 to 1971
55. William Gorham	Horsehandler 1976	85. Tom Merino	Packer 1940
56. Chris Grimes	Packer 1985	86. Mark Messinger	Packer 1987 to 1988
57. Delyn Grube	Packer 1982 to 1983	87. Richard Meyerhoff	Packer 1981
58. Ted Hammond	Packer 1974	88. Robert McCloud	Packer 1947
59. Robert Hannum	Packer 1975	89. William McDaniel	Horseshoer 1931
60. Kenneth Hanville	Packer 1935 to 1936	90. Floyd McFarland	Packer 1936
61. Merrill Hanville	Packer 1938	91. Bob McGregor	Packer 1932 to 1938
62. George Harders	Packer 1985 to 1986	Bob McGregor	Packer Foreman 1939 to 1969
63. Jerry (Paco) Harlow (N.A.)	Horseshoer 1986 to 1988	92. Frank McWhorter	Packer 1962 to 1967
64. Frank Hendricks	Horseshoer 1918	93. David L. Miller	Packer 1952
65. Jack Hoxie	Packer 1942	94. Jess Mitchell	Packer 1938
66. Jon Jessen	Packer 1952	95. John Moe	Packer 72 to 74, 86 to 87
67. J.H. Johnson	Horseshoer 1931	96. Steve Moore	Packer 1984
68. Brent Johnson	Packer 1978 to 1981	97. David Morgan	Packer 1972
69. Charlie Johnson (N.A.)	Packer 1941	98. Ed Morgan	Packer 1958 to 1959
70. Dan Jones	Packer 1974, 75, 80, 88	99. James Mosier	Horsehandler 1978
71. Roger Kahl	Packer 1948	100. Forrest Murphy	Packer 1940, 1950 to 1967
72. F.W. Kassabaum	Packer 1931 to 1932	101. Charles Olsen	Packer 1958
73. Frank Keeler	Packer 1970 to 1872	102. Carlos Ortiz Jr.	Packer 1966 to 1970
74. Kermit Kirk	Packer 1982 to 1985	103. Barry Palo	Horsehandler 1978 to 1979
75. Korwin Kirk	Packer 1981 to 1985	104. R. (Sweet Pea) Patterson	Packer 73 to 81, 85 to 88
76. Dan Kirn	Horsehandler 1986	105. A.E. Pehl	Packer 1923
Dan Kirn	Packer 1987 to 1988	106. John Peters	Horseshoer 1931 to 1932

107. Everett D. Philip	Packer 1938	134. Don Utley	Packer 1986
108. F.N. Prairie	Packer 1922	135. Andy Van Riper	Packer 1921
109. Donald Pugh	Packer 1951	136. Richard Waring	Packer 1979 to 1985
110. Kermit Randoor	Packer 1987 to 1988	137. Kenneth Wass	Packer 1963 to 1968
111. Mike Richardson	Packer 1970 to 1975	138. Ralph Wass	Packer 1962 to 1967
112. Bud Rickey	Packer 1960 to 1961	139. Rick Watson	Packer 1971
113. Craig Ritchie	Packer 1983 to 1984	Rick Watson	Horseshoer 1972 to 1980
114. Karl Rowe	Packer 1980	140. Jamie Watts	Packer 1985
115. Joe Rube (N.A.)	Packer 1917 to 1941	Jamie Watts	Horsehandler 1984
116. Bradley Ruble	Packer 1979 to 1988	141. William Welch	Packer 1927, 28, 31 to 38
Bradley Ruble	Horsehandler 1975 to 1978	142. Arch Westfall	Packer 1933 to 1939
117. Roy Rust	Packer 1917	Arch Westfall	Ranger 1930 to 1932
118. Pat Sanchez	Packer 1956 to 1957	143. Waine B. Westfall	Packer 1949 to 1955
119. Michael Schoedel	Packer 1981	Waine B. Westfall	Horseshoer 1956 to 1963
120. Wyle Selby	Packer 1951	144. Waine E. Westfall	Packer 1918
121. Robert Slater	Packer 1987 to 1988	Waine E. Westfall	Ranger 1916, 1922, 1923
122. Robert Stickles	Packer 1949, 1950	145. Robert Westmoreland	Packer 1985 to 1986
123. Abe Subia	Packer 1975 to 1981	146. William Wholley	Packer 1939
124. Daniel Sousa	Packer 1939	147. Steve Wight	Packer 1956, 1957, 1960, 1962
125. Joe Souviewski	Packer 1927	148. Harold Williams	Packer 1935 to 1936
126. Joe Subler	Packer 1956 to 1957	149. Kenneth Williams	Packer 1966 to 1971
127. Frank Sutton	Packer 1936	150. Merle Williams	Packer 1954 to 1955
128. Fred Tappin	Packer 1955	151. Clair Wolfsen	Horseshoer 1950, 1952 to 1956
129. Matt Taylor	Packer 1978	152. Bob Woods	Packer 1972
130. Ron Taylor	Packer 1975 to 1976	153. Wells Woolstenhulme	Packer 1938 to 1940
131. Flavial Tomlinson	Packer 1941	154. Steve Ybarra	Packer 1982 to 1985, 1988
132. Joe Trabucco	Packer 1940	155. John C. Cox (Cecil)	Packer 1947 to 1954
133. Joe Thibodeau	Packer 1960		

TEAMSTERS

1. W.E. Abbs — 1923
2. W.W. Adams — 1925
3. Carl Allen — 1923
4. E.S. Allem — 1925
5. Ralph Anderson — 1923
6. Erwin Ashworth — 1923
7. George Ashworth — 1922,23,26
8. E.L. Atkinson — 1925
9. Clifford Aultman — 1927
10. Ray Austin (N.A.) — 1918-1931
11. B.E. Barmore — 1922
12. Rodney Bays — 1922,23,25
13. A.W. Beach — 1926,1927
14. Joseph Bekert — 1925
15. F. Beal (N.A.) — 1916,1921
16. Carl Beckland — 1918
17. O.D. Biddle — 1925
18. W.A. Blanchard — 1924, 1925
19. Harry Blockwell — 1925
20. V.V. Boggs — 1925
21. Fred Bolender — 1921
22. Ed Bouchard — 1917
23. A.E. Bowen — 1924
24. B. Bramlett — 1923
25. Adam Bricker — 1921
26. John Breen — 1920,1921
27. W.H. Breuner — 1925
28. H. Bridges — 1917
29. Jack Bridges — 1925
30. Fred Briggs — 1919
31. C.C. Britton — 1918
32. J.J. Brown — 1922
33. John Brown (N.A.) — 1917
34. Floyd Brown — 1924
35. Roy Brown — 1924
36. Russell Brown — 1922
37. W.M. Brown — 1915
38. W.F. Brown — 1925
39. G.W. Bryan — 1925
40. B. Buck — 1927
41. George Bullock — 1920
42. R. Cabezut — 1925
43. V. Cacy — 1925
44. Joe Callahan — 1924
45. E.H. Cantrell — 1925
46. W.B. Cantrell — 1919
47. D.R. Carlon — 1916
48. R.H. Carlsen — 1919
49. G. Cartwright — 1922
50. J.W. Chadwick — 1925
51. Charles Chapin — 1920
52. E.D. Chiles — 1925
53. W.H. Clark — 1924
54. William Clark — 1919

55. John Clark	1921	86. George Easom	1918-1924
56. Henry Clenford	1922	87. Jay Easter	1918
57. Frank Coleman (N.A.)	1916-1918, 1921	88. John Ege	1924, 1926
58. Tom Coleman	1918	89. C.V. Ellis	1916-1919
59. Wm. T. Coleman	1921	90. F.J. Elwell	1916-1919
60. J.E. Collins	1922-1925	91. L.C. Elwell	1919
61. John Conneally	1926	92. A.V. Emmert	1922
62. J. Conway	1918	93. H.A. Ewing	1925
63. T.O. Cook	1925	94. W.S. Farnsworth	1925
64. Wm. J. Court	1920	95. E. Fay	1925
65. Frank Craig	1923	96. Jas. Finley	1919
66. John Craig Jr.	1924	97. B. Fisher	1925
67. David Crane	1924	98. Clinton Fleming	1915, 1916
68. Charlie Cronin	1917	99. James Fleming	1916
69. E. Cunningham	1925	100. Ray Flynn	1918
70. F. Curran	1918	101. W.F. Footman	1922
71. K.D. Curran	1925	102. G.T. Foust	1918
72. G.B. Curtin	1916, 1917	103. Phillip Frayne	1925
73. E.C. Darley	1925	104. Richard Fromm	1923
74. Wm. Dakan	1924	105. H. Gallagher	1915
75. J.R. Davey	1925	106. Joe Garcia	1918
76. M.C. Davis	1926	107. A.C. Gibson	1915
77. Ray DeGroon	1924	108. Ed Gilbert	1919
78. George DeHarte	1918	109. Russell Gilpin	1924
79. Peter Delphia	1918-1922	110. A.W. Ginn	1925
80. George Dexter	1915	111. Charlie Gooch	1925
81. George Dieter	1916	112. E. Gordon	1915-1924
82. H.R. Doherty	1917	113. P. Gordon	1917-1923
83. P.J. Dooley	1922	114. Frank Grace	1922
84. W. Driscall	1920	115. L.J. Haflick	1923
85. Jerry Dunn	1919	116. C.S. Hall	1923

117. T. Halliman	1916	148. O.C. Jackson	1923
118. L. Halstead	1924	149. Thomas Jackson	1925
119. Paul Hamilton	1915	150. Albert Jerrery	1917
120. F. Hammond (NA)	1922	151. A. Jernstad	1926
121. W. Harkness	1925	152. C.O. Johnson	1920
122. Wm. Harrington	1922	153. F. Johnson	1920
123. B.H. Harris	1923	154. C. Johnston (NA)	1919
124. Chas. Harris	1918	155. Harry Johnston	1925
125. Paul Harris	1921	156. Frank Jones	1918
126. Edgar Haskell	1918	157. Hugh Jones	1921
127. Thomas Hayes	1925	158. Jean Jones	1915
128. Henry Hedges	1917	159. Presley Jones	1924
129. J. Henderson	1919	160. A. Kamensky	1920
130. F. Hendricks	1918	161. J. Keating	1917,18,20
131. W. Hibpshman	1919,1922	162. E.G. Kehoe	1920
132. C. Hibpshman	1922-1925	163. John Kelley	1924
133. F.W. Hill	1915	164. E. Kelly	1925
134. Samuel Hinkle	1925	165. John Kemp	1921
135. Harold Hjort	1923	166. Pete Kennedy	1925
136. Henry Hoffman	1923	167. A.J. Kercher	1924
137. H. Hogan (NA)	1920,21	168. A.J. Kyle	1925
138. Wm. Hogan (NA)	1921	169. L. Lagowarsino	1917
139. J. Holland	1924-1927	170. J. Lague	1919
140. R.A. Holliday	1925	171. A.J. Larken	1925
141. Frank Hollis	1922	172. A. Larsen	1923
142. G.W. Howard	1923	173. Sydney Ledson	1924
143. L. Howell	1922	174. Harland Lee	1923
144. John Howlett	1919	175. Fred Lemons	1925
145. H.R. Humphfries	1925	176. J. Leonard	1921-1924
146. E.C. Hunt	1922	177. John Levey	1927
147. O.A. Huseboe	1921	178. Henry Lewis	1923

179. J. Lindsey	1916-1918		210. R.M. Nielson	1925
180. W.P. Locke	1918		211. J. Nolan	1926
181. J. Lofitus	1922		212. J.W. Nolan	1925
182. Edwin Mann	1923,24		213. J. Noonan	1912
183. John Manning	1919		214. Francis O'Neill	1922
184. Jeff Marshall	1921		215. Thomas O'Neill	1923
185. Frank Martin	1918		216. P. O'Shaughnessey	1920
186. R. Martin	1925		217. W.H. Otterson	1921
187. Wm. Martin	1919,25		218. J.D. Owen	1925,26
188. Noel Mays	1917		219. Robert Pace	1924
189. G. Mentzer	1916-1921		220. Joe Parolovich	1925
190. Gus Meyers	1925		221. F. Penny	1925
191. R. McCarn	1919,24,27		222. C.F. Peregoy	1926
192. J. McCready	1920-1925		223. Charlie Peregoy	1925
193. C.C. McCumber	1923		224. E.W. Perry	1923
194. Bert McDole	1918		225. A.L. Pettis	1915,16,22
195. B.D. McGettigan	1925		226. J.S. Phillips	1925
196. James McGibson	1925		227. W.H. Phillips	1922
197. W. McGlynn	1917		228. C.W. Pierson	1925
198. F.J. McGowan	1918		229. George Pope	1920
199. R.J. McKinney	1925		230. Walter Pratt	1925
200. Wm. McNamara	1918		231. L.W. Renolds	1925
201. J. McNeil	1922		232. Mike Riodan	1923
202. H.D. McRenolds	1922		233. J.B. Roberto	1923
203. J. McSwain	1915		234. R.O. Robson	1924
204. Tom Miles	1918		235. Arthur Rosen	1923
205. A.C. Miller	1924,25		236. Joseph Ross	1926
206. J.H. MIller	1922		237. Chas. Rouse	1918
207. W.J. Moffett	1925		238. Jack Russell	1924
208. J. Morgan	1923		239. Jesse Rust	1916,17
209. R.J. Munn	1916,17		240. Harry Sauve	1921

241. Francis Sawyer	1925	272. J. Trumbly	1915-1926
242. Wiber Sawyer	1925	273. Jack Tomick	1925
243. C. Schloff	1921	274. Jessie Turner	1922
244. M.E. Seeley	1923	275. Wade Turner	1922
245. G.E. Shasteen	1923,24,26,27	276. E. Vanciel	1923
246. Jack Shaughnessey	1926	277. Joe Vanciel	1922
247. F. Shaw	1924,26,27	278. A. Van Riper	1923,24
248. Fred Shaw	1923-1925	279. Moses Varain	1918
249. R.W. Shaw	1915-1931	280. L.V. Wade	1925
250. Irwin Shilling	1923	281. C.J. Walker	1916
251. Art Shimer	1919	282. C. Wallace	1919,1923-1927
252. J. Shimer	1917-1924	283. W.S. Wallace	1925
253. Heney Shortt	1922	284. William Wallace	1923
254. Dan Siefried	1919	285. G.H. Warne	1918
255. A. Skeleton	1916-1924	286. George Warren	1915,16
256. C.Z. Smith	1915-1922	287. A.S. Watts	1917,18,22
257. F.J. Smith	1925	288. C.A. Weathers	1926
258. Sam Snover	1925	289. Wm. Welch	1927
259. Charles Snyder	1919	290. Ben Wenger	1917
260. W. Stanford	1923	291. Henry Westfall	1924
261. D. Stockton	1923-1925	292. W.E. Westfall	1924
262. William Straw	1921	293. Alfred White	1917
263. Harvey Sutton	1923	294. E.R. White	1922
264. A.R. Tarbox	1925	295. Joe Wiffler	1923
265. C.W. Tedrow	1912,1916,1917	296. Andy Wilds	1925
266. Joe Tedrow	1915-1922	297. J.B. Williams	1923
267. L.F. Tedrow	1916	298. James Williams	1925
268. Alf Thompson	1925,1927	299. Tom Williams	1925
269. Casey Thurman	1921	300. Harry Wilson	1920
270. D.F. Thurston	1922-1925	301. J.D. Wilson	1925
271. Duff Truitt	1925	302. James Wilson	1923

303.	Wallace Wilson	1923	308. Wm. Wormley	1920
304.	C.S. Winans	1918	309. Harry Wright	1924
305.	B.E. Winger	1918	310. J.B. Wyman	1923
306.	Arnold Wolff	1915	311. F.L. Yancy	1919
307.	Clair Wolfsen	1924	312. L.A. Yates	1926

NPS Army Mules of 1957

1. Bob
2. Pappy
3. Dan Patch
4. Bernadine
5. Marilyn
6. Stover
7. Carson
8. Ike
9. John
10. Jake
11. Tiger
12. Red Man
13. Little Red
14. Buck
15. Maizie
16. Whitie
17. Colorado
18. California
19. Clara Belle
20. Sorrel
21. Lois
22. Babe
23. Socks
24. Billy
25. Coalie
26. Blue
27. Brownie
28. Janie
29. Belles
30. Spot

Pate Valley Trail - 1921

www.ingramcontent.com/pod-product-compliance
Lightning Source LLC
Chambersburg PA
CBHW040004040426
42337CB00033B/5221